ZEN
and the
ART
of
HOUSEKEEPING

*The path to finding meaning
in your cleaning*

LAUREN CASSEL BROWNELL

A**dams**media
avon, massachusetts

Published by
Adams Media, an F+W Publications Company
57 Littlefield Street, Avon, MA 02322. U.S.A.
www.adamsmedia.com

ISBN-13: 978-1-59869-449-9
ISBN-10: 1-59869-449-9

Printed in Canada.

J I H G F E D C B A

Library of Congress Cataloging-in-Publication Data
is available from the publisher.

This publication is designed to provide accurate and authoritative information with regard to the subject matter covered. It is sold with the understanding that the publisher is not engaged in rendering legal, accounting, or other
professional advice. If legal advice or other expert assistance is required, the
services of a competent professional person should be sought.

—From a *Declaration of Principles* jointly adopted by a Committee of the
American Bar Association and a Committee of Publishers and Associations

Many of the designations used by manufacturers and sellers to distinguish
their product are claimed as trademarks. Where those designations appear in
this book and Adams Media was aware of a trademark claim, the designations
have been printed with initial capital letters.

*This book is available at quantity discounts for bulk purchases.
For information, please call 1-800-289-0963.*

To my husband Malcolm,
who has always believed in my crazy dreams,
and to my children,
Wyatt and Gabby,
who inspire me to keep dreaming them.

CONTENTS

ACKNOWLEDGMENTS

In her terrific novel *Goodnight Nobody*, author Jennifer Weiner gives life to lead character Kate Klein, a suburban wife and mother who tries to solve a murder while her kids are at preschool—between 9 and noon on Monday, Wednesday, and Friday. I wrote this book in much the same way. The reading, writing, and research required for this book were completed in stolen moments—bits and pieces— middle of the night revelations—notes scribbled at stoplights and transposing my scribbled notes during my daughter's nap time. It became like my third child—a being that had to have lots of attention and whatever one-on-one time I could spare. And I loved every minute of the time spent with it.

Thanks go to my precious children, Wyatt and Gabby, and my stepson Casey. They make it worthwhile to try to be a better person in every sense of the word. Thanks to my parents, Sue and Jay Cassel, who have spent a lifetime loving me and supporting me in *every* endeavor. They taught me to love learning and to love words. I could never have undertaken this project without their support and the background they provided for me. Thanks as well to my wonderful parents-in-law, Malcolm and Mildred Brownell Sr., who have spent the last ten years loving me and supporting me in *every* endeavor.

To the Zen Friendz—I couldn't have done it without you girls! Special thanks to Emily Noble, Stacie Conner, and Cindy Blackwell. Y'all are my nearest and dearest even though you're all more than 500 miles away! And to my aunt, Verna Wood, who knew that someday I would be ready for *Gift from the Sea*.

I am so grateful to Colleen Sell and Indi Zeleny, who by including my work in theirs made me believe I had a story worth telling (Sell is the editor of the bestselling *Cup of Comfort®* series and Zeleny edited the innovative anthology *Herstory: What I Learned in My Bathtub . . . and More True Stories on Life, Love, and Other Inconveniences*). I owe a large debt of gratitude to Paula Munier and Brendan O'Neill at Adams Media for providing me this opportunity and the guidance to make it happen.

And to Malcolm, thank you seems inadequate. I love you today, tomorrow, and always.

INTRODUCTION

The best time for planning a book is while you're doing the dishes.
—Agatha Christie

The concept for this book came to me while doing the dishes. Who would ever have thought that I would have something in common with the great mystery writer Agatha Christie? But there I was, elbow deep in soapsuds, bemoaning my fate with every slide of the sponge across the plate, when something (or someone) from somewhere said to me, "You have to do it. Why fight it?" A feeling of calm came over me in that moment unlike any I've ever known. It was like that stereotypical view of seeing your surroundings in slow motion when a character in a movie "gets it"—when the concept that "he really loves her" or "she's really been a workaholic and now wants to make things right with the ones that she loves" dawns on him or her for the first time. With dish soap bubbles popping around me, I looked at my children. I was doing this for them. I realized I was hurrying to finish the dishes so the kitchen would look nice when my husband got home. I was doing it for him. And seeing clearly at the end of that day there was no place on earth I would rather be than in that kitchen, with those kids, waiting for that man to come home, I realized that I was doing it for me as well.

On the evening of my dishwashing epiphany, I started thinking about the importance of being right where I was. Of not wishing away these small moments that make up my life. I also thought about the generations of homemakers of which I was now a part. I realized that at that moment there were literally hundreds of thousands of women doing exactly what I was doing. And then I began to ponder the *millions* of women who had come before me, who have done this work of keeping a house for hundreds, if not thousands of years.

As keepers of the home, we have an incredible opportunity to make an enormous impact on the quality of the lives we live and the lives of those that we love. This impact can best be felt by doing small things well—the things that make life worth living, that give our existence its depth and its richness. In my case, I may not be bringing home the bacon. But I am the one who knows exactly how much mayo to put on the bread of each and every member of my family in order for them to have the perfect BLT. I may not be in a laboratory finding a cure for skin cancer. But I am the one that puts sunscreen onto baby shoulders. Should I bemoan my fate? Or should I cherish my place in the world and ponder the enormity of its intimacy? While washing those dishes, I made the conscious decision to choose the latter, and that choice led me to the path of Zen.

Prior to my life as a full-time wife and mother, I was a newspaper sales and marketing executive. I then spent several years as a sales trainer, traveling the country to guide newspaper advertising sales staffs to personal and professional success. Part of my programs focused on time management and organizational skills. I was a classic example of "Do as I say—not as I do," and at times I felt a bit like a fraud. But I shared good information and helped people along the way. Since beginning my Zen journey, however, I am much more authentic. I will not share anything in these pages that I have not experienced for myself. If it can work for me, it can work for you as well.

Some people argue that approaching housework as a path to enlightenment is not plausible. Erma Bombeck, one of the first women to look at the humorous side of housekeeping and raising a family, which she wrote about in her syndicated newspaper columns and numerous books of essays, once said, "Cleanliness is not next to godliness. It isn't even in the same neighborhood. No one has ever gotten a religious experience out of removing burned-on cheese from the grill of the toaster oven." My aunt Verna Wood of Albuquerque, New Mexico, says, "Zen and housekeeping are mutually exclusive—you will never reach enlightenment through housekeeping."

These women are worldly and wise, but with all due respect, I have to disagree with them. I think enlightenment *is* an achievable goal and I think housekeeping is as potentially powerful an avenue for its attainment as any. Whether she knows it or not, I think my Aunt Verna does too on some level. After swearing that one will never find enlightenment through housework, she went on to say, "I try to think of housekeeping as a short mental vacation—let my mind freewheel like I do on a walk or a swim. I sometimes come up with solutions to problems I didn't even know I had." If that's not enlightenment, then I don't know what is. And Zen itself is tricky like that. The profound power of its simplicity will sneak up on you and before you know it, you are intuitively implementing its principles and benefiting from its practice.

Throughout this book, you will find helpful hints and guide-posts that will assist you in both understanding and implementing the concepts discussed. Each chapter will begin with a "cleaning koan" for contemplation. A *koan* is basically a Zen riddle. It is a question or statement that has no right or wrong answer but can be used as a tool for focusing your thoughts when meditating. Pondering these thoughts is ideally supposed to help one find enlightenment. The koans offered at the beginning of each chapter are designed to help you contemplate the deeper, richer meaning of what occurs in the rooms of your home and the sig-

Buddha says . . .
"Better than a thousand hollow words is one that brings peace."

nificance of dedicating yourself to the cleaning of that space or to completing that specific household duty. It is through imbuing these daily tasks with deeper meaning that we begin to embrace the power of Zen.

"Living One with Nature" will provide you with "recipes" for creating your own nontoxic and inexpensive household cleansers.

Living one with nature is an integral part of practicing a Zen philosophy. "Zen Homemasters" are real quotes from real women who are facing and embracing the challenges of keeping their homes. "Seeds of Rapture" are immediately applicable and/or critical ideas to implement into your cleaning practice, and in "Buddha Says . . ." segments you will see firsthand the philosophical concepts that are the basis for Zen practice. At the close of each chapter you will find a "Try This" exercise to help you explore that chapter's concepts more fully and implement the ideas discussed. A mantra for meditation and a haiku close each chapter. Both are tools designed to assist you in making forward progress toward enlightenment. A *mantra* is a concise word or phrase repeated over and over during meditation to focus your mind and energy. Try mine or create your own. *Haiku* is a form of traditional Japanese poetry consisting of three lines; there are five syllables in the first line, seven in the second, and five again in the third. Creating haiku is an attempt to reduce complex concepts to their most basic form and express the magic of any given moment without relying on tools that we consider necessary for poetry such as similes, metaphors, or rhyming words. Punctuation is not important either. Just words that clearly express the feelings or actions of a moment in time. They are lots of fun to write. Give it a try!

We will also apply the *seven factors of enlightenment* to specific household tasks. These seven factors, much like koans, mantras, or haiku, are meant to be concepts for contemplation that can lead you toward enlightenment. In Buddhist teaching, the factors of enlightenment are part of the practice called *Wings to Awakening.*

Embrace and implement them, in housekeeping and in life, and ultimately they will guide your spirit to flight. These factors are *investigation, tranquility, mindfulness, concentration, energy, equanimity, and rapture.*

Unwittingly, we utilize these seven factors many times throughout the course of a given day and they are especially applicable to incidents that occur regularly in our households. Let's say that while you are out of the room, a bunch of multicolored goldfish crackers mysteriously make their way to the living-room floor, are walked all over or wrestled on, and are now making a beautiful and crunchy mosaic of your carpet. You are *mindful* as you become aware that the goldfish are indeed in a million miniscule pieces on the floor. You *investigate* why this has occurred. Something like, "Who in the hell left these goldfish on the carpet?" should do the trick. You continue the investigative process as your children point fingers and cast blame on each other, a litany of imaginary friends, and finally the dog. Once you get to the bottom of the mystery, you utilize your *energy* to either (a) place the offending child in time out or (b) lug the vacuum cleaner from the hall closet. Once you take a deep breath and rationalize that the carpet really did need to be vacuumed anyway, *tranquility* begins to flow through you (a bit of a stretch, but work with me here!). You *concentrate* your efforts on sucking the goldfish out of the rug and at last, you find a certain *equanimity.* The situation irritated you but its resolution was relatively quick and reasonably painless, your carpet looks better, and you have one less item on tomorrow's "to do" list. With the situation resolved, you look into the eyes of your precious progeny (and the dog) and realize you wouldn't want to live your life any other way. At that moment you have worked your way through the seven factors of enlightenment to arrive at a place of *rapture*—a moment of pure and unadulterated joy. Divine? No. Applicable to the challenges of housekeeping and daily life? Absolutely!

Zen and the Art of Housekeeping will serve as your guide as you look at your home through fresh eyes. You'll learn the basic principles of Zen and how to effectively integrate them into what will become a more positive and rewarding housekeeping experience. My goal is to help make cleaning your home easier, by changing the way you look at the work you do around your home as well as providing useful and usable tips and techniques that I have learned through the time-tested teacher: trial and error. By implementing the ideas you find here, you will have a more fulfilling experience in your cleaning. It is my hope that you will also begin to incorporate some of the Zen concepts that we explore here into other facets of your life. Applying Zen to the cleaning of my home was simply a starting place. These principles have wound themselves into many aspects of my life, making me feel more peaceful and relaxed and at the same time making me feel empowered with the awareness that I am all that I need to be, that what and who I am are just fine. Regardless of the tasks that must be performed, I have the right to feel whole and content as I walk and work through my day-to-day life. The good news? So do you!

zen concept

all things in
moderation

cleaning koan

does a house have
buddha nature?

ONE.

THE MIDDLE WAY

*A*well-known koan and one often assigned to newer practitioners of Zen is "Does a dog have Buddha nature?"
It's an interesting thought to consider, similar to our Judeo-
Christian debate over whether or not animals have souls. Consider
this question and its application to housekeeping. Is a house a living entity? Does a house have Buddha nature?

My conclusion is that a house is the ultimate in Buddha
nature. One of the essences of Zen teaching is nonattachment.
A house is not attached to its occupants at all. *We* are attached to
it. A house simply is—it exists to serve very important functions
at the present moment. It has a past but doesn't obsess over it. It
may or may not have a future. A house exists fully in the present
moment to protect us from the elements, gives us a place to keep
our "stuff," and provides us a place to come together with friends
and family. Keeping a house clean should not be an issue that is

charged with emotion, and yet most people are passionate in their attitudes toward keeping house. They either love it or they hate it. There is no in between! How have we allowed an inanimate object, our home, to inspire such strong feelings? We are fighting against the healing powers of Zen when we allow the care of our home to get the best of us. In Zen, everything simply is what it is, and it is exactly what it is supposed to be. Certainly we want our home to be beautiful and welcoming, color coordinated, and clean. But it is *our* wants, needs, desires, style, and taste that we project onto our home that give it "personality." A true personality is something that only a living being projects. Homes do not have their own personality. They reflect ours.

This is why the Zen approach to living *The Middle Way* is so very important. The Middle Way encourages us to practice all things in moderation. When it comes to household chores, we need to let go of the extremes of love and hate, do the work that needs to be done, and be perfectly present in every moment.

WHO WAS BUDDHA ANYWAY?

Buddha was not a god. He was an ordinary man on an extraordinary quest to find the deepest possible meaning in his existence. After being born into wealth and privilege and finding no answers behind the walls of his father's palace, he determined that a life of excess was no way to find meaning. There must be another way! He tried to find enlightenment by embracing suffering, by doing without all material possessions, and he nearly starved himself to death in the process. And yet, still no answers to the questions of life. So it was that he decided that it was a life lived in moderation, the Middle Way, which would provide the best basis for the pursuit of enlightenment.

Buddha's journey to enlightenment took him six years, culminating in a marathon stretch of meditation under a *bodhi* tree, during which he determined the nature of existence and became an "enlightened one," a Buddha. My journey has taken a lot longer than six years. Actually, it is a journey that we all begin again each day. The most meaningful discovery you can make as you begin to internalize the concepts that will help you become a Zen Homemaster is that in order to have any hope of finding enlightenment, you must come to terms with the place that you call home.

EVERY JOURNEY BEGINS WITH A SINGLE STEP

Our parents bring us "home" from the hospital, and thus begins our lifelong relationship with our homes. As we journey toward adulthood, we begin to develop certain attitudes about the tasks required to maintain our homes. It is only when we venture out on our own, however, and have the opportunity to express ourselves completely in our own surroundings, that we really discover what our style of making a home will be.

My homemaking journey began after I graduated from college and took a job in a management training program that took me from my parent's home in Austin, Texas, to Wilmington, Delaware, and the first apartment that I could truly call my own—no parents within thousands of miles, no prefabricated dorm room furniture, no roommates. Just an empty third-story apartment that beckoned to be filled. And fill it I did. With a white sofa and matching love seat. A beautiful butcher-block dining table. Art that moved me. Books that I loved. As I learned about myself, free from the expectations and eyes of others, I also learned about my taste in furniture, how I wanted to use my space, who I wanted to invite into my life and my home, and how I wanted to keep house.

Buddha says . . .
"It is better to travel well than to arrive."

Back then it was easy. And it remained easy for many years as I traveled and worked and could keep my house any way I wanted and only had to clean up after myself. Then I met the man I would eventually marry, and we began to mesh our lives together. Over the course of the next several years, we developed our careers, accumulated belongings, and became the parents to two beautiful children. And life got messy—literally and figuratively.

Just as Buddha's journey took him from riches to rags and ultimately to enlightenment, I have journeyed from dependence on my parents to total independence to interdependence with the members of my family. We are a system—an organic entity that is ever-changing and evolving. One of my main roles in the structure of this family is to be the one who does the majority of cleaning. I have undergone a journey in that respect as well.

Cleaning up after myself was not a big deal and if I didn't feel like doing it I didn't have to. As life got fuller, richer, and more complicated, it was no longer okay to just say "I don't like to keep house!" The problem was I truly hated housekeeping. There was so much work to be done to maintain my home. Trying to keep all the disparate souls under my roof happy and trying to maintain some level of control over the multiple activities that took place there each day was a monumental task. My journey was complicated by the fact that the nature of my husband's work caused us to move frequently. I zigzagged across the country trying to set up house in one place after another, never feeling particularly connected to any one place and having the sense that my life was always about either packing or unpacking boxes.

At long last, though, I have found peace. Life didn't get simpler. Quite the contrary. As my children grow, as I mature, as my husband and I come to a new place in our relationship, life is getting more complicated. We didn't quit moving. We have lived in our current location for a year and a half. It won't be long before it is time to pursue the next opportunity for advancement, and chances are that will be a long way from Lubbock, Texas. The answers did not come from without. They came from within. I had the answers all along; I was just unwilling or unable to see them. I found my place of peace by reprioritizing and learning to live fully in the present, appreciating my life as it exists in this moment, and keeping housework in its proper perspective—living the Middle Way.

LIVING THE MIDDLE WAY

In contrast to our present extremes of emotion about housekeeping, there are all shades of gray in living the Middle Way. There are opposite ends of the cleaning spectrum, neither of which will lead us to a place of peace. At one end of the spectrum is the neat freak, wanting to exercise total control over his or her environment. Cindy Woods, a marketing professional in the telecommunications industry and divorced mother of two once existed at this end of the cleaning spectrum. She says, "Through my teen and early adult years, I used neatness and perfection as a control in my life when I could not control my unhappy feelings. I used to be an obsessive neat freak, but that was just an outlet for my unhappiness." Luckily, Cindy has been able to find the Middle Way for herself. She explains, "I am now engaged to a wonderful, loving man who is the soul mate I never knew and will marry him in the spring. Yes, life does give you a second chance. Now, I like things somewhat in their place but I am not going to break out in hives or fall down with a heart attack if they are not. It is *much* more important to live life, be happy, and enjoy your loved ones than it is to live in a cleanliness shrine."

At the other end of the spectrum is the slob, a label that has been applied to me on more than one occasion. I have asked myself repeatedly, "Why am I like this?!" Why is the simple task of keeping a house so incredibly disdainful? As I began my journey to enlightenment, I went looking for answers.

Scientists trying to understand the workings of the human brain have discovered that, to a large extent, we may be born with a predisposition to cleanliness or sloppiness. Stacie Conner, a homemaker and mother of two from Newtown, Pennsylvania, said during a recent conversation, "I don't know how some people can keep a house spotless 24-7. I guess they are just born that way." Apparently, Stacie may be right. We are each born either right- or left-brain dominant. The two hemispheres of the brain control different actions, behaviors, and thought patterns. The most visible representation of left- or right-brain dominance is whether someone is right- or left-handed, but the differences go much deeper.

Left-brain people like to color inside the lines and usually enjoy keeping house. They are logical and analytical. The right-brained people of the world prefer to scribble on the walls and are okay with disorder. They tend to be creative and more abstract in the way they approach problem solving. The functionality of our brains also impacts the way we approach frustration. As humans, it is an innate desire to avoid frustration, but neat freaks and slobs do it differently. The slobs of the world want to avoid frustration *now*. Their mantra is "I'll do it later." They take off their shoes as they come in the door and leave them there, drop wet towels on the floor for a later laundry day, and pile dirty dishes in the sink because they don't feel like washing them right now. In contrast, the motivating force for a neat freak is to avoid frustration *later*. They don't take off their shoes until they get to the closet, they take the wet towels to the laundry room and start a load of wash, and they wash dishes as they go.

The following real-life scenario is indicative of the behavior pattern of a typical right-brain-dominant homemaker, one who wants to avoid current frustration, is easily bored, and is seemingly unruffled by clutter and disorganization:

You arrive home from the grocery store around 2:15, get most of the groceries out of the car, but leave bags of nonperishables in the trunk to be unpacked later. Eggs and milk go in the refrigerator while the rest of the groceries are left in their bags on the counter and scattered on the kitchen floor. You pick up the kids from school, do homework, and send them outside to play, all while weaving through the obstacle course of unpacked bags of groceries. Then the witching hour arrives. It's five o'clock and you find yourself in a race against time to get everything put away and dinner started before your husband arrives home.

Whose scenario is this? You guessed it! Yours truly. Much of my life was lived in this state of disarray. Many evenings my husband arrived home to a highly emotionally charged environment that was all of my own making. I was uptight and harried, the kids could sense it, they began to act up, I began to freak out, etc. This is no way to live and it is certainly not a pathway to peaceful living. All this can be avoided simply by following each task through to completion and accepting a few minutes of inconvenience now in order to avoid a great deal of headache and heartache later.

One positive to being an innately messy person is that we tend to be a lot of fun. We are caring and kind and we love to play games. Unfortunately, the games we play are often with ourselves, games like "How long can we stay away from the house?!" Sylvia Kelly, an executive with the Louisiana Department of Transportation, mother of three grown children, and stepmom to an eight-year-old, has played this game a time or two. Sylvia shares, "When my children were small, we were always on the go with ball games, dancing, and gymnastics—anything to keep from going home to a dirty house." If you can't leave your house, there's plenty of fun to be had right under your own roof!

Jamie Sumlin, an artist, marketing professional, and mother from West Monroe, Louisiana, shares my affection for sleeping through prime housecleaning time. "Always take naps," Jamie suggests. "The house does not seem so messy."

Probably the most personally destructive game we avid antihousekeepers play is transference of the negative feelings we have about our homes. You know something is wrong but you don't know what it is. You feel unfulfilled. It must be my husband! It must be the kids. I must need to get a job. I must need to quit my job. You have this uncomfortable feeling that you simply don't fit in your own skin. The life you were meant to live is out *there* somewhere. As writer Gertrude Stein stated, "There is no there there."

Zen Homemasters

"I have friends that are crazy at keeping their house. When I need to feel clean, I leave and go to *their* house."

Karla Hopf
Operations manager and
mother of two
Bensalem, Pennsylvania

When Buddha attained enlightenment, what he discovered was that these feelings of discontent are one element of existence common to the human condition. In other words, almost everyone feels this way at one time or another. We all suffer. We all experience what the local Zen Master would call *dukkha*. Our search for enlightenment is really a search for a solution to why we suffer and how to avoid it. *The Four Noble Truths* offer this guidance.

The First Truth that Buddha discovered is that we all suffer. The Second Truth tells us that we feel these feelings of discontent because of desire. We want what we can't have. We are constantly trying to keep up with the Joneses. The very thing that will make us happy is consistently just beyond our grasp. The Third Truth explains that we can eliminate our dukkha by eliminating desire. The Fourth Truth defines how to ease desire and thus ease our suffering. The Eightfold Path that Buddha defined (see sidebar) provides us a road map for how to live our lives in a way that will provide us with peace and contentment, and it is this lifestyle that is the practice of Zen.

Sometimes, regardless of the functioning of our brains, the way we are raised has a stronger impact on the way we keep house than our natural instincts. Cindy Blackwell, a professor of journalism at Oklahoma State University, is one of the most creative people I know. She's also one of the most organized. Many aspects of her work and personality would lead you to the conclusion that she is a right-brain-dominant person and thus would tend to be a bit of a slob. So how does she overcome her natural tendencies? She explains, "My father is a marine and my mother is an accountant. What more can I say?"

The Eightfold Path

In order to ease personal suffering and journey toward enlightenment you must practice:

Right understanding
Right thought
Right speech
Right action
Right livelihood
Right effort
Right mindfulness
Right concentration

You can also find yourself rebelling against the way you were raised. Many of the women I spoke with said they either grew up with excessive disorder so they became really good housekeepers, or they grew up in homes where you couldn't touch anything because it might get dirty. Some of these women swore to themselves that their homes would not be so rigid and so they tolerate greater disarray.

We each have different strengths, weaknesses, and problem-solving skills. Just as our koans have no right answer, there is no *one* way of living. We must respect our differences and honor our uniqueness. The uptight and analytical among us can learn to loosen up and have more fun. The fun-loving game players of the world *can* create beautiful homes without losing any of their zest for life. Zen tells us that each of us is spectacular and unique—the only one of us that there will ever be and that we are perfect just as we are. Work within the framework that already exists in your life and face a little frustration on occasion. It works wonders!

Zen Homemasters

"Type A personalities have to struggle with everything not being perfect in the house. It's sometimes more important that my kids get attention or that we leave the home calm and relaxed. I have had to balance my own need for order with other needs."

—*Heidi Anne Mesmer*
Assistant professor at
Oklahoma State University
and mother of two
Stillwater, Oklahoma

UNPACK THOSE BAGS

For whatever reason, there is a lot of psychological baggage connected to housekeeping. Some experts feel that a messy house is a sign of low self-esteem, the result of a homemaker who doesn't believe he or she deserves to live in nice surroundings. Others explore the concept that living with disorder is a way of acting out in a passive-aggressive manner. This usually occurs when you don't receive the support of those around you. Outwardly you put on the façade that everything is okay, but your actions don't match your words.

Another piece of baggage that is psychologically connected to our housekeeping practice is what I have dubbed *perfection paralysis*. You begin to hold yourself up to unreasonable standards and rather than fail to achieve the perfection you seek, you subconsciously choose to do nothing at all. It can be very eye-opening to realize that the pursuit of perfection is pointless and in direct opposition to the principles of Zen. In Zen, we seek to understand that with all our human imperfections, we are as nearly "perfect" in any given moment as we will ever be. What we are right now is just fine. The condition of our homes is just fine as well. Can we aspire to more? Absolutely. But the goal of Zen Housekeeping is not to have a home that is perfect. It is to embrace the *process* of keeping the house—one perfect moment at a time.

The Amish are well known for the beauty and quality of their handmade quilts. The patterns are so intricate and the stitch work so fine in its detail that each quilt transcends its usefulness and becomes a work of art. And yet, in the process of creating each quilt, one piece of fabric that does not match the others exactly, or one group of stitches unlike the others is included, a tangible reminder that only God is capable of truly perfect creations.

HOW OTHERS PERCEIVE THE
"DOMESTICALLY CHALLENGED"

For most of us who have or have had less than ideal cleaning practices, we fear that others will judge us negatively because of our less than perfect environments. Instead of motivating you to overcome your challenges, this fear actually paralyzes you and you find yourself living in complete and utter CHAOS. Cyber cleaning queen "The Fly Lady" created the CHAOS acronym, which stands for Can't Have Anyone Over Syndrome. But are people really judging us so harshly? Bad news. Apparently they are.

It is very common for people to make assumptions about others based entirely on the cleanliness and/or organization of their homes or workspaces. In the research study *Is Cleanliness Next to Godliness? The Role of Housekeeping in Impression Formation*, Drs. Paul B. Harris and Daniel Sachau "conducted a study to determine if the cleanliness of an apartment would affect observer impressions of the resident." The answer to this question was a resounding yes. The Sachau and Harris study determined that those who are perceived to be inadequate housekeepers "received lower ratings on measures of Agreeableness, Conscientiousness, Intelligence and Femininity."

Environmental psychologists have long been studying theories of human territoriality, the concept that the way we treat the spaces that we occupy and call our own reveal a great deal about who we are. In their study, Drs. Harris and Sachau expound on the ways in which our feelings about ourselves are reflected by our homes. The way we decorate and care for the environments in which we live and work shouts loudly to the outside world about our internal identity. Additionally, the more care and maintenance we give to our living spaces the more attached we become to them and the more deeply ingrained our sense of belonging becomes. We are happier and healthier if we have clean and pretty homes.

In her book *Biting the Dust*, Margaret Horsfield confirms that right or wrong, the state of our homes is a barometer by which other people measure us. According to Horsfield, a poorly kept home has long been "associated with poverty and disease." A well-kept house is indicative of "high values and wholesome living." Because it is the woman who is the primary keeper of the home, these judgments are applied to her as well.

This concept of packing your psychological baggage and carrying it with you through the entirety of your life is inherently Western in nature. However, as we have already seen in our discussion of dukkha, Zen philosophy does acknowledges the fact that there are concepts that may come between you and enlightenment and that it is better to acknowledge and address them than to try to ignore them. They are called the *Five Hindrances*, the first of which, *desire*, has already been introduced. Let's look briefly at these roadblocks and how they steer our journey toward domestic bliss off course.

THE FIVE HINDRANCES

The first and immensely powerful hindrance, *desire*, can be managed through the practice of gratitude and awareness that all that you have and all that you need are yours right now. As it relates to housekeeping, you want to maximize the beauty and livability of the space you have at this moment. As you vacuum your carpets, for example, if you spend that time wishing you had better-quality carpets in a house that was 4,000 square feet bigger and situated on the French Riviera, you have missed the moment of loving all that is yours, that you have worked hard for, and that more than adequately provides for you and your family. You not only dislike the act of vacuuming, but you walk away from the process of it more discontented and disheartened than when you began.

Anger is the second of the five hindrances, primarily negative feelings directed toward others. I have spoken with some women that claim that when they are ticked off, they turn into cleaning machines. But this is not a path to enlightenment. It may result in shiny surfaces, but it is detrimental to you from the inside out and to those you love from the outside in. If the only way you can get your children to clean their rooms is by yelling at them, how do you think they are going to feel about one day cleaning their own homes? How willing are they going to be to lend assistance to you? Practicing Zen doesn't mean that you are never going to get angry again. We are all human, and life is full of challenges. Some of those challenges are going to make you really mad! Living in the moment with Zen simply encourages you to express that anger at the moment that it is appropriate. Don't bottle it up for later and allow it to eat away at your happiness or poison acts that can and should be done in a spirit of harmony—such as maintaining your home.

Sloth is defined as halfhearted action with little or no concentration. I guess you could call it just plain laziness. It is tough to come to terms with the fact that you just might be a bit lazy, but accepting yourself, warts and all, is part of the path to Zen. The best way to address the issue of "laziness" is to allow time for it. Turn this hindrance on its ear by giving your full concentration to your housekeeping and investing completely in the actions in which you are engaged. Use lazy time as a reward. Once your tasks are complete, watch a chick flick, take a nap, read the latest issue of *Cosmopolitan*. If you are practicing all things in moderation, living the Middle Way, there is a place for rest and relaxation. You just can't allow sloth to be the undoing of your good intentions.

Buddha says . . .
"Holding onto anger is like grasping a hot coal with the intent of throwing it at someone else; you are the one who gets burned."

Worry is worthless and it has no place in the life of one practicing Zen philosophies. It doesn't do any good anyway. The vast majority of things you worry about will never come to fruition and worrying about them is simply a trick that your mind plays on you—forcing itself into a future that is unknown. When worry overtakes you, you get so caught up in your head that it is difficult to function effectively. You become paralyzed and stuck in a moment that will probably never come. Action in the present moment is the cure for worry. Ask yourself what positive step you can take right now to ensure that good things come your way. Just as negative thoughts feed on themselves, positive thoughts multiply in just the same way. If you absolutely can't calm the inner workings of your mind and free yourself from worry and anxiety with a positive action, sit down and breathe deeply for a moment. Figuratively invite the worry to come in and have a seat with you. What is the root of this worry? Why is your mind going down this negative path? Is this really the issue that is of concern or are you transferring feelings about something else? If you think better with a pen in your hand, get out your journal and write in the middle of the page, "What am I worried about?!" Draw lines out from the center and jot down everything that comes to your mind, or make a list of all that is currently concerning you. Sometimes embracing what troubles you is the only way to rid yourself of its hold on you. However you do it, get to the bottom of it and then get back to what you were doing. This hindrance can sidetrack you from the work you need to do only if you let it.

The last of the five hindrances is *doubt*. Do you ever doubt your abilities? Doubt your intelligence? Doubt the feelings another has for you? Doubt

> *Buddha says . . .*
>
> "There is nothing more dreadful than the habit of doubt. Doubt separates people. It is a poison that disintegrates friendships and breaks up pleasant relations. It is a thorn that irritates and hurts; it is a sword that kills."

is another mind game that your inner voices like to play with you. They want to keep you questioning yourself just enough that you won't give them a permanent eviction notice. Doubt is simply you not believing in you. The elements of Zen that we will explore here are all designed to build a strong foundation of trust in yourself.

WARNING: IT MAY GET WORSE
BEFORE IT GETS BETTER

As you begin implementing Zen practices into your daily life and particularly into your housekeeping rituals and routines, you will most assuredly experience a period of transition. Things may seem in greater disarray than ever. Your head may feel full of thoughts even though you understand on an intellectual level that what you are trying to achieve is a state of clearing your mind. You may have particularly vivid dreams. This is all part of the process and should be expected and embraced. You are laying the groundwork for peace to flow. Consider the words of English historian Dame Cicely Veronica Wedgewood, who said, "Discontent and disorder are signs of energy and hope, not despair."

Keep moving forward. You are at a critical juncture in your life's journey—coming to terms not just with dirt and disorder but quite possibly patterns that you have been practicing your entire life. Don't get discouraged. And don't let the input of others deter you. I can almost guarantee that at some point in the initial stages of your Zen journey your significant other will say, "I thought you were supposed to be cleaning." Your kids will whine, "Why can't we just do it the old way?!" Just smile knowingly. They will see soon enough how much better life can be. Then take the next step in your journey.

Initiating your journey down the path of Zen Housekeeping leaves little room for excuses. Regardless of which hemisphere of your brain is dominant, no matter what your psychological hang-ups may be, scientific psychological research supports what your spirit knows intuitively. It is time to get real, get busy, and get control of your home.

DEVELOPING A SYSTEM

After much personal trial and error, the one way that I have found for achieving the state of *equanimity* (one of our seven Zen factors of enlightenment!) that we seek is by developing a system. For me, the system that works best is a written schedule of tasks to be performed each day. I talked to dozens of women about their feelings and attitudes about housework, and almost all of those who were at peace with their housekeeping practices had a system of some sort in place—some ground rules by which they played the game of life.

A system is not something that is written in stone. It is merely a framework within which to work. Without one you will most likely feel that housework is a never-ending trial that must be endured. "Just when you think you're through, you look around, the dust bunnies have multiplied, the toilets have ring around the collar, and your daughter's soccer socks have the whole washroom in an uproar," says Denise, a full-time homemaker who shared her thoughts on housekeeping with me. Julie Wilbur, a full-time mom and part-time piano teacher from Stillwater, Oklahoma, really enjoys the maintenance of her home. She says, "I actually love 'housekeeping'—making order out of chaos feels good. What does not feel good is having the rest of the family push so hard to get things back to chaos again. I feel like it is never-ending, and I don't just mean that when dishes get dirty you have to wash them again. I mean that I am constantly spending time doing the same chores over and over because other people won't help me. There are lots of projects I would like to do, but it takes all my energy (and more) just to keep us from being buried in a pile of stuff."

With a system in place, you will see that there is a clearly defined beginning and end to housework that ultimately frees you to enjoy the many other pleasures that life holds. It also helps keep housework in its proper perspective and places realistic limits on the time we dedicate to it.

In 1919, Christine Frederick, a pioneer in the study of the domestic arts, wrote a textbook and designed a correspondence course for homemakers, both titled *Household Engineering*. In the book, she addresses the need to develop a housekeeping system, stating, "The whole idea is simply, plan what you are going to do, do it, and then rest; instead of not knowing what you are going to do, resting or stopping when you feel like it, and never knowing when you are going to get done."

Frederick believed that we should all devise a written set of instructions for the maintenance of our homes, a set of Standard Operating Procedures. Her theory was that the reason most women could cook so much better than they could clean was because one followed a written set of instructions, a recipe, when cooking. If you had written instructions for the maintenance of your home, you could be just as successful. When it comes to cooking, the more you do it, the more comfortable you become. You gain confidence. You know what works and what doesn't. You develop shortcuts and more efficient and effective ways of completing the tasks required to prepare a meal. It is the same with cleaning. Creating and implementing a personal cleaning system and allowing it to serve as the recipe for caring for your home will help eliminate the frustrations you feel, make the tasks seem less daunting, and allow you to embrace your responsibilities more objectively. If you are just beginning your Zen Housekeeping journey or if you want to revamp your current system to improve its efficacy, a written schedule can be a tremendous step in the right direction.

The first step in developing your schedule is to make a list of all the tasks that must be accomplished in order for your home to run smoothly. There are three categories that most household chores will fall into: daily maintenance, weekly tasks, and seasonal or annual projects. For the moment, we are primarily concerned about the daily and weekly duties—the recurring work that is required to keep our house at a certain level of cleanliness and organization. We will further explore seasonal and annual projects in a later chapter. Remember, our focus at *this* moment is on the *present* moment.

For many of us, our life dictates a lot of what our cleaning schedule will look like. If you work outside the home, evenings and weekends are going to automatically be the time for you to schedule your home maintenance responsibilities. If you work at home or are a full-time homemaker you will have a bit more flexibility in your scheduling. Thus, within the constraints of your life, create a schedule that is SMART!

Specific: Make your schedule as **Specific** as possible. What are you going to do and when are you going to do it? The more precise you are in assigning time to housekeeping, the more likely you are to succeed and the more freedom you will feel from housekeeping constantly hanging over your head.

Measurable: How will you **Measure** your accomplishments? What is your acceptable standard of cleanliness? How will you determine that you are "finished"? Where does housekeeping fall on your personal list of priorities? One of my goals is to be free from major housekeeping duties over the weekend. You still have to engage in your daily maintenance tasks and again, if you are employed outside the home, the weekends may be the only time you have to clean. Regardless, applying a way to measure the success of the attainment of your housekeeping goals will make them tangible and ultimately far more achievable.

Attainable and Realistic: Your schedule of tasks should be **Attainable** and **Realistic.** Having a home that is always spotless and free from clutter is, for most of us, unattainable. Is it realistic to put washing your windows, inside and out, each week on your schedule? If you set the bar too high you are setting yourself up for failure. If you create a housekeeping system and it fails, you will be right back at the beginning of the process, discouraged and despondent. You can also overorganize yourself and the members of your family, making your system so complicated or rigid that you can never maintain it. Don't fall into this trap.

Timely: Your schedule should also be **Timely**. At this point in the process, don't worry about your goals for next year's spring-cleaning. There's time for that later. What can you do today, tomorrow, and maybe next week to get yourself on the right track?

As you begin to create your cleaning system and schedule, review it regularly to make sure that it is SMART: specific, measurable, attainable, realistic, and timely.

Sample Housekeeping Schedule

By way of example, this is my housekeeping schedule:

Monday: 9 A.M. until 11 A.M., make all beds; sweep and mop 3 bathrooms and kitchen; scrub bathrooms, showers, and commodes. 7 P.M. until 8 P.M., clean kitchen and bathe children.

Tuesday: 9 A.M. until 11 A.M., make all beds and pick up all clutter and toys and vacuum all carpets. Noon until 3 P.M., laundry. 7 P.M. until 8 P.M., clean kitchen and bathe children; pick up all clutter before bedtime.

Wednesday: 9 A.M. until 11 A.M., make all beds, dust all surfaces, and work on miscellaneous projects (straightening closets, clearing clutter, cleaning out garage, etc.). 7 P.M. until 8 P.M., clean kitchen and bathe children; pick up any clutter before bedtime.

Thursday: 9 A.M. until 11 A.M., make all beds, pick up all clutter, and wipe down bathroom surfaces. Afternoon, work on miscellaneous projects, like weeding the flower beds or other outdoor projects. 7 P.M. until 8 P.M., clean kitchen and bathe children; pick up any clutter before bedtime.

Friday: 9 A.M. until noon, make all beds and complete all laundry before the weekend. 7 P.M. until 8 P.M., clean kitchen and bathe children; pick up any clutter before bedtime.

Notice that in my schedule, Mondays are pretty full. I enjoy getting the bigger projects out of the way early in the week. Additionally, I do most of my cleaning in the mornings. I am a morning person and feel most energetic and motivated to do physical activity before noon. I have small children at home and have to leave time for writing and other work projects. This schedule leaves most of my afternoons free so that while little ones nap, I can settle down at the computer for some quiet contemplative time. The physical work of maintaining my house is out of the way, and often I find that while I have been doing my housekeeping in the morning, an idea has come to me that I want to explore in my afternoon writing sessions. Consider the rhythm of your life as you begin creating your schedule.

Honor your own internal clock as you create your cleaning schedule. In order to follow it, your schedule has to work for you. Is getting up a few minutes early or staying up a few minutes after others go to bed going to be the most effective way for you to do daily maintenance? Do you need everyone else to be out of the house or is your ideal schedule one that involves teamwork?

BEGINNER'S MIND

Approach the development of your housekeeping schedule with what Zen Master Shunryu Suzuki calls *shosin*, or "beginner's mind"—seeing everything related to keeping your home as if you were seeing it for the first time. Let go of your preconceived notions about cleaning house. Erase the negative messages that play in your mind like, "I am a crummy housekeeper" or "I would rather have a root canal than clean the bathroom."

This is an opportunity to start fresh and find meaning in your relationship with your home and the work that must be performed for its maintenance. Your most powerful cleaning tool is not your vacuum cleaner. It's not your dishwasher or even your maid! It's your brain. If you are consistently and relentlessly feeding yourself negative messages about how

Zen Homemasters

"You just kind of develop a routine, complete each room before moving to another one, and try to think happy thoughts."

—*Dee Dee Halpain*
Homemaker and
mother of two
Lubbock, Texas

much you hate to clean, of course you're going to dread it. Your mind does not differentiate between negative thoughts and negative actions. They are both equally powerful in your mind's eye. Therefore, flipping the switch in your head from negative feelings to positive ones about household maintenance can be the key to embracing the tasks more fully and enjoying the process more.

"In the beginner's mind there are many possibilities,
but in the expert's there are few."
—*Shunryu Suzuki*

What if you could alter your thinking so profoundly that instead of terrible torture that must be endured, you could look at cleaning as a rewarding experience? How enlightening would that be? Using the profound power of our mind to refocus our energies toward the ultimate positive outcome and not the interim drudgery is a fantastic stepping stone on our path to Zen.

DON'T PUT OFF UNTIL TOMORROW . . .

Procrastination is one of our least productive habits both personally and professionally. When you put off difficult tasks to be accomplished at some later time, whether you are cleaning your home, making a difficult phone call, paying your bills, going to the gym—whatever—the difficulty of the task grows in direct proportion to the amount of time you delay acting on it. "I'll do it later" is the phrase that serves as one of the greatest obstacles between you and Zen Housekeeping. These four little words will always steer you off course. Live in the moment, act in the moment, and don't be afraid to tackle the tough jobs first.

Eating a frog for breakfast is the most effective tool I know for avoiding the stress caused by procrastination.

Zen Homemasters

"There is something different about the energy in a clean house. It's refreshing, welcoming, relaxing . . . peaceful. The result of the effort makes the effort not seem like such a chore. Cleaning house visually pays off very quickly. In a way, it's an accomplishment that can be repeated on a regular basis."

—*Penny Pennington*
Assistant professor
Oklahoma State University
Stillwater, Oklahoma

If you do the thing you most dread first, everything else seems much easier by comparison. I have a collection of frogs—stuffed

Seeds of Rapture

While there is no need to put it in black and white on your written schedule, keep in mind that it is allowable (and advisable) to have some fun while you are keeping house. Turn the music up loud. Sing at the top of your lungs. Light some candles. Anything to make the moment more enjoyable.

frogs, ceramic frogs, silver frogs, you name it—placed strategically around my house. Members of my staff gave them to me when I was a sales trainer and advertising manager. I would always remind them to "eat a frog for breakfast" each day, and all these various frogs began to appear mysteriously in my office. Now that the course of my life has changed from a sales manager to a manager of my home, the frogs still remind me to tackle the tough jobs first and eat a frog for breakfast. Frogs for breakfast are really not so bad! In fact, the French consider frog legs a delicacy!

MAKE A MASTER LIST

Used in conjunction with your housekeeping system, a Master List can make life much easier. It is like a "to do" list on steroids, where on a single sheet of paper you list everything you can possibly think of that needs to be done. Your Master List should include not only things to be done immediately but also longer-term projects, things that you want to do but may or may not ever get around to, and life goals. It should also include things as trivial as items to pick up at the grocery store. Absolutely everything. There is nothing too big or too small to go on your Master List. Keep your list with you at all times. It should be updated each week, so it's helpful if you can create your list on the computer, adding and deleting items as you accomplish them, think of new projects to add, or change priorities. If a computerized list is not an option, it can certainly be done by hand. Simply copy the undone items to your new list and leave off the ones that have been accomplished.

A Master List is such an effective tool because it eliminates the need for multiple calendars, grocery lists scribbled on the backs of envelopes, Post-it notes with phone numbers for future reference, and the like. If you're waiting in line at the drive-through of the pharmacy, pull out your list and see what needs to be done next. While in the middle of a meeting you remember that you need a birthday card for Aunt Sally. Pull out your Master List and jot it down. It is a snapshot of your life in one portable place, and even if you have a tendency toward disorder, your Master List can keep you on top of things, at the right place at the right time, and can keep your little corner of the world running smoothly.

Zen Homemasters

"Housekeeping is much more fun with an iPod! Sometimes I swear with an iPod I could clean forever. And at times, housework is great therapy because of the instant gratification."

—*Joann DeLucia*
Mystery shopper and newlywed
Mercerville, New Jersey

You can also use your Master List to assist you in creating a plan for tackling errands geographically. On the frequent days of your life when it feels as if all you are doing is running errands, you can spend a great deal of time and a whole lot of gas going back and forth across town. Look at your list and consider what you have to do in a day and then place these tasks in order grouped by location. With time being your most precious nonrenewable resource and gas at $3 a gallon or more, thinking through what you need to accomplish and developing a plan of attack can be a lifesaver.

TRY THIS

Make a visit to a nearby stationery store and pick out a journal that you will use specifically for developing your housekeeping system and charting your progress in the pursuit of a cleaner home and a clearer mind through Zen. Select one that speaks to you and your sensibilities. Set aside some time to walk around your house as an unattached observer. What needs the most attention? Where are trouble areas? What is already working well? Where do the frogs lurk? What do you postpone? Look at your life and the commitments that are already in place that must be worked around as you devise your system. What time are you willing to commit to the requirements of cleaning your home? What are

Living One with Nature

Homemade All-Purpose Cleaner: Mix one part water with one part vinegar in an empty spray bottle for an all-around disinfectant and deodorizer. No, your house will not smell like a salad bar. The vinegary smell dissipates as it dries. Do not use straight vinegar. It must be diluted with water or it will be too acidic to serve your purposes.

your goals? Journal about the reasons *why* you want to begin your Zen Housekeeping journey. Review all that you have written and create your schedule. Implement it for one week and then return to your journal. What worked? What didn't? What did you forget to include in your original? It may take a few weeks for you to work the kinks out of your system, but once you've got a system going that works for you, you can put your cleaning on autopilot knowing that you have laid the groundwork for coming to terms with the tasks around your home. Try to schedule a few minutes each day for quiet contemplation. During this process you may want to use the following mantra and/or haiku to lend focus to your meditation.

mantra for meditating on the buddha nature of the home

Show me the path to bring light and love to this home.

housekeeping haiku

mine in this moment
honoring this home and hearth
spirit of love resides

zen concept

meditation

cleaning koan

if the kitchen is the heart
of the home, what is the
heart of the kitchen?

TWO.

THE HEART OF THE HOME

*O*ffer the above koan to three different people for consideration and you're apt to receive three different answers. You can make the argument that the stove is the kitchen's heart because it is the place where you create the food that nourishes not only bodies but souls as well. Or maybe the table is the heart of the kitchen. It is the place set aside for the coming together of all the disparate souls that live under one roof. But I believe that the woman of the house is the heart of the kitchen. She is the one that infuses the kitchen with purpose and passion, that makes it a warm and welcoming place, and it is her presence that calls others to congregate there.

And boy do they congregate! How many parties have you attended where regardless of theme, occasion, age of guests, and so forth, everyone has eventually migrated to the kitchen? The kitchen is where families gather, meals are shared, and often, where bills are paid, homework is done, and family meetings are held. The kitchen is the most frequently utilized and visible part of most homes and, of course, it is where all food is prepared. Therefore keeping our kitchens clean is critical, for both our health and our happiness, and should be at the top of our list of cleaning priorities.

---

*"The here, the now and the individual have always been
the special concern of the saint, the artist, the poet, and—
from time immemorial—the woman."*
—*Anne Morrow Lindbergh,* Gift from the Sea

Just as the kitchen is the heart of the home, meditation is at the heart of the practice of Zen. Although Buddha studied other religions, traveled extensively, and sought the guidance of both religious leaders and commoners alike, it wasn't until he immersed himself fully in his practice of meditation that he received enlightenment. In order to fully embrace a Zen approach to cleaning your home, you need to first develop an understanding and appreciation of the power of meditation and mindfulness.

MEDITATION

No other room in your home requires as much work to maintain as the kitchen. By the same token, no other room offers so many rewards as that of a clean kitchen. It is the same with meditation. For many of us, with our extremely busy lives and constantly buzzing minds, meditation may seem an extraordinarily difficult concept to master. But the rewards will be worth it.

Zen practitioners seek to find enlightenment through clearing their minds and connecting to a higher level of clarity and thought. The main way this enlightenment is achieved is through the daily practice of meditation. The image that comes to most of our minds when we think about meditation is traditional *zazen,* or sitting meditation. Traditionally, those practicing zazen will place a mat on the floor and a round cushion on top of that and sit in lotus pose, with legs crossed in front and each foot resting on the opposite thigh. Lotus pose is meant to emulate the perfection of a lotus flower and provide the ideal physical circumstances for focused awareness. However, Zen, and therefore meditation, is not about following rules and regulations, so if lotus pose is uncomfortable or just doesn't work for you, sit another way—even sitting in a chair is acceptable. It is far more important that you free yourself from distractions and work on the mindfulness and self-discipline that you will gain from meditation.

Once seated in a quiet place and a comfortable position, your focus should turn to your breathing. Don't try to make it do anything. Just breathe and pay attention to your breath and try to think of nothing else. Your mind may wander, your feet may cramp, and your internal monologue (or dialogue if you like to converse with yourself) may kick into high gear. When you feel yourself tuning into these distractions, acknowledge it and then retrain your focus back to your breath. There is no preset amount of time that you have to sit in order for your meditation to work, but you should sit still and quiet long enough for your heart rate, your breathing, and your mind to slow down. As you become more experienced, you will be able to meditate effectively for longer and longer periods of time. For now, the emphasis should be on beginning the process and planting the seeds of future growth as a practitioner of meditation.

The benefits of zazen are numerous, and I encourage you to try to find a few moments each day to practice this proven "prescription" for reducing high blood pressure and stress, and more importantly, just for improving your own personal happiness and well-being. For our purposes in pursuit of a clean home and a way of getting that home clean that will embrace Zen principles, we will more often need to practice another form of meditation—*kinhin*—walking meditation.

In kinhin, you are simply continuing many of the methods used in your seated meditation and taking its implementation on the road. Zen Masters will often intersperse periods of kinhin with their zazen practice, still focusing on their breathing and the clearing and focusing of their minds while they are in motion. You can practice kinhin while walking down the streets of your neighborhood, through a nearby park, or as you go through your daily duties. At this point, you may be thinking that you have enough trouble walking and chewing gum at the same time. How are you ever going to be able to clean house and meditate? You are attempting to achieve a focus and an awareness of what you are doing in any given moment of kinhin practice.

Seeds of Rapture

Be in the moment fully. Experience it. Embrace it. No matter what that moment is.

Housekeeping kinhin can include noticing the way your shoulder muscles contract and expand as you mop the floor of the kitchen. While vacuuming, a Zen Homemaster practicing kinhin might make note of the patterns on the carpet that the Hoover leaves behind. She will take note of the fragrance of the lavender essential oil she has sprinkled in her dishwater and hear the quiet hiss of the steam as it escapes from her iron and smoothes the wrinkles from the clothing of her family. She will no longer view housework as drudgery, but will learn to welcome it as an opportunity to involve all her senses and soothe her spirit as she cares for her home. If we think about each moment of our lives—every task that must be done, every meal that must be made, every diaper that must be changed—as a form of meditation, these tasks begin to take on a profound importance. Each of these acts becomes part of a much larger whole and we become an integral part of something bigger than ourselves.

"Meditation is simply about being yourself and knowing about who that is. It is about coming to realize that you are on a path whether you like it or not, namely the path that is your life."
—*Jon Kabat-Zinn, author of* Wherever You Go, There You Are

Zen Masters feel that the key to achieving enlightenment through meditation is its *daily* practice. Our minds and bodies will resist this move toward discipline and so we must show them

Buddha Says . . .

"To enjoy good health, to bring true happiness to one's family, to bring peace to all, one must first discipline and control one's own mind. If a man can control his mind he can find the way to Enlightenment, and all wisdom and virtue will naturally come to him."

the way by incorporating this process into our existing daily routine. What else do homemakers, housekeepers, and housewives do daily? They clean, they cook, they care and nurture. If each act becomes a quest for peace and enlightenment placed in its proper perspective, each day can become a celebration and not a "to do" list that must be endured. Buddha said that "good deeds done with selfish intention are useless for gaining enlightenment." What act of housekeeping can you think of that is purely selfish in nature? We benefit from the acts by having clean clothes, pretty homes, soothing suppers. But primarily, these acts are to better the lives of those we love and thus they align perfectly with the path to enlightenment that we can seek through Zen.

Seeds of Rapture

Don't get stuck in a rut! This applies to both Zen and to housekeeping.

- Do you usually practice kinhin? Try a zazen session instead.
- Move your meditation practice outside or to a different location in your home in order to push yourself further along the path to enlightenment.
- If you find that you always clean the rest of the house first and never get to your bedroom, do the opposite and start with your room first next week.
- Do you always start your cleaning with the guest room and bathroom because it takes the least amount of effort? Try saving it for last the next time you clean. Reward yourself with the easiest job at the end of the process.

FAST TRACK TO ENLIGHTENMENT?

As you review the housekeeping schedule that you created in Chapter 1, what chore absolutely and almost without exception requires daily practice? Cleaning the kitchen! In fact, if you are anything like me, your kitchen probably requires multiple cleaning encounters each day. If we make the kitchen a place of meditation and mindfulness, we will ensure that we are practicing our Zen daily as well. Since necessity requires multiple kitchen cleanings each day, can we fast-track our path to finding peace? Unfortunately, we probably won't achieve enlightenment any faster just because we clean our kitchens frequently. Enlightenment arrives in its own time, not in ours. However, we may find a more peaceful existence by truly using kitchen cleaning time to its fullest.

My kitchen is such a busy place that it seems to be in almost constant use. On weekdays, I make breakfast for my children each morning and pack their lunches. Since I work at home, my husband often comes home and joins me for lunch. Afternoon snacks segue directly into dinner preparation. Weekend mornings call for fun, festive big breakfasts, busy weekend days usually require a light lunch of soup or sandwiches, and my husband and I love to try out new recipes or old-fashioned favorites for weekend evening meals. So most weeks, I literally have three meals a day, seven days a week to prepare (not to mention plan and shop for). That's a minimum of twenty-one golden opportunities to get in touch with the heart of my home. And that does not even take into account cooking special treats with your kids, preparing food for parties, holiday baking, or making something for a church or office potluck.

In addition to its extensive usage, cleaning your kitchen is an interesting combination of short- and long-term cleaning projects, which make it a particularly challenging area to keep clean. There is the aforementioned cleaning up after each meal, which includes tasks such as washing the dishes and wiping down countertops. But there are also more appliances "per capita" in the kitchen than any other room in the house. Defrosting refrigerators, cleaning ovens, maintaining the microwave and stovetops, all require regular applications of elbow grease. Arguably, no other room in the house requires so much thought, planning, and effort.

MEDITATION IS SELF-CLEANING
FOR THE SOUL

Consider the self-cleaning cycle of your oven. You turn it to the appointed cycle and leave it alone for a while to do its thing. You then come back later and wipe it down. With your "frost free" refrigerator, you first have to clean out all the accumulated junk that has been stored in there. Then you turn off the power and leave the doors open so the icebergs that have built up within can melt away. Meditation—just taking a few quiet moments and sitting quietly, breathing deeply, thinking about a specific concept or, ideally, thinking about absolutely nothing, or moving through your tasks in a state of mindful awareness—works in just the same way. It "self-cleans" your body, mind, and spirit. No one else can do it for you, but it allows you to walk away from the world for a few moments, just as you walk away from the oven or the fridge as the work there continues on its own. Meditating doesn't make your work or your life effortless, but it puts you a step ahead. It helps you to get rid of the junk that accumulates in your mind, weighing you down, stressing you out, and making you sick or tired or sad. After a few minutes of meditation you do have to

Living One with Nature

- Cut a lemon in half, sprinkle it with baking soda, and use it as a "sponge" to wash your dishes. It can also be used to eliminate stains on countertops.
- Scrub your sinks with baking soda. It will remove stains and freshen the smell of the drain.
- Run vinegar through your coffee pot instead of water to remove stains.

return to the world you left, just as you have to return to the oven and freezer. But you return rejuvenated, ready to face the task, calm and centered, and at peace with your place in the world.

While it is patently un-Zen to multitask, when it comes to maintaining your home, it only makes sense to utilize small pockets of time to their full advantage. These pockets of time are abundant in the kitchen. Unload the dishwasher in the time it takes to microwave a frozen dinner. While something simmers for its recipe-required fifteen minutes, sweep the floor, load the dishwasher, or do a quick load of dishes, and jot down staples that you need to pick up from the grocery store while you are running errands tomorrow. No matter how many tasks your body may be performing, set your mind free. Let go of work worries. Don't spend the time balancing your checkbook in your mind. Just be. In that space. In that place.

EASING DUKKHA THROUGH DISHWASHING

Most of our household appliances are godsends. Without them we would be beating our clothes against rocks and having ice blocks delivered by a horse-drawn buggy. The dishwasher is the one appliance most people think they can't live without, as doing dishes is the chore that has to be done most frequently in the majority of homes. However, if you rely completely on your dishwasher to do all the dirty work of cleansing bowls, plates, pots, and pans, you are missing out on one of the great contemplative opportunities that housekeeping has to offer.

Hand-washing dishes is very effective and when experienced fully can be extremely rewarding on a spiritual level. It is a moment of mindfulness that is there for the taking. There are few if any other household chores that so completely integrate all of our senses. Instead of cursing your fate when you have a handful of items that simply will not fit in the dishwasher, try celebrating your good fortune instead. Or make it an evening ritual to put all the dishes in the washer and hand-wash your pots and pans. Run a sink full of soapy, sweet-smelling, warm-to-the-touch water. Fully appreciate the sights, smells, and sounds. Watch the soap bubbles pop as you part the water with your hand. The repetitive motion of the sponge across the plate can become almost hypnotic. It is a sweet experience for the senses as well as for the soul. Consider the shape, weight, and feel of each item as you soap and rinse it. Where did each piece come from? Was that plate part of a place setting that was a wedding present from Aunt Mabel? Did you purchase that set of glasses on a fun-filled day of shopping with your oldest and dearest friend? The chip in that plate—when did that get there? Engage in the experience. Your troubles will flow down the drain as quickly as the dishwater.

TOP TO BOTTOM

When you're cleaning your house or when you are practicing Zen, it is most effective to work from top to bottom. This is particularly true in the kitchen. You don't want to invest the time and energy to sweep and mop the floors and *then* wipe down the countertops, brushing crumbs onto your already clean floors. Meditation works the same way. You start at the top, clearing your head and freeing your mind from its predictable pathways of worry or anxiety. As you learn to relax your mind, your body will follow suit.

At the end of a long day, and particularly if you prepared the meal as well, the last thing you want to do is clean the kitchen. Cleaning as you cook makes the task much less daunting. But even if dinner dishes have not yet been cleared away, it is worth the time and effort to end your day with a clean kitchen. Why is this so important? Because what you accomplish the night before lays the groundwork for the next day. Walking into a dirty kitchen and a sink full of dishes takes the wind out of your sails immediately. It is almost impossible to fully explore the Zen experience if you are walking into a space that is already holding so much negative energy. No matter how good your intentions are for having a great, productive day, it is difficult to overcome the bad feelings that a dirty kitchen will instill in you. Chances are, you will let it stay that way, get worse, and hang over your head all day. If you invest just ten or fifteen minutes in the evening, you are free to begin the next day without that burden. You can also get into bed with the positive feeling of accomplishment that cleaning the kitchen will instill. Load the dishwasher and start it, wash whatever is left by hand, and wipe down the countertops. If you are a coffee drinker, one of the best things you can do for yourself is purchase yourself a pot with an automatic timer. Set your coffeepot up so that a fresh cup of coffee will be waiting for you in the morning, sweep the floor, and finally, rinse out the sinks, turn off the light, and call it a day.

Seeds of Rapture

Never go to bed with a dirty kitchen. Following this one recommendation faithfully can have a dramatic impact on the quality of your life and the cleanliness of your home.

COUNTER CULTURE

Once upon a time, kitchen countertops were almost all the same—predictable plastic laminate in a variety of colors—and their care was relatively straightforward. Not so in today's kitchen and cooking-crazed culture. The plethora of possible materials that can grace today's countertops require that we look at a few countertop-cleaning ground rules.

Plastic Laminates

The primary reason that plastic laminate countertops are being replaced by other materials is that while they do provide the cook with a smooth working surface, they are not very durable. They scratch and stain easily and they are very susceptible to damage from heat. Ideally you should use nonabrasive cleaners. A soft sponge and a liquid cleaning solution should be about all that you apply to these counters to clean them. If you have this type of counter surface you should also have plenty of hot pads and cutting boards on hand. Never place a hot pan or dish directly on them and do not use them as a cutting surface either. The scars will show and they are impossible to remove. Wipe up any spills immediately to prevent staining.

Ceramic Tile

The *tiles* of a ceramic tile countertop are tough as nails, virtually indestructible, and wonderfully resistant to heat. However, the grout that holds the tiles in place is not nearly so tough, so you have to treat those seams gently. Use a soft toothbrush to clean the grout directly if it is stained. Look at the labels of kitchen counter cleaners and find one that is safe to use on both the tile and the grout in between.

Marble and Granite

These beautiful and durable materials are being used regularly in building today's homes and remodeling kitchens. Their rich color and shine bring a touch of elegance to the kitchen and they stand up well to the heat. They are porous, however, and will stain if they are light in color, so wipe up spills immediately with a damp sponge or rag. Highly abrasive cleaners can damage their shiny finish or leave small marks that will dull their shine, so except for the worst spills, just wash with warm water and buff dry.

COOKING AS CONTEMPLATION

Some people feel about cooking the way I used to feel about housekeeping: It is simply a headache they don't need. If you want a clear-cut pathway to Zen, however, there are few household activities that are more rewarding than the preparation of a good meal. Give it a try! Enjoy the colors of the vegetables as you chop them, the aromas of simmering pots, and the smiles on the faces of happy family members after they enjoy a meal you lovingly prepared. If you cook, you can also use this fact as leverage and leave kitchen cleanup for someone else. It's a win-win all the way around.

When my husband and I were dating and then newlyweds, cooking dinner together was our favorite pastime. We would get home from work, change clothes, and meet in the kitchen for a cocktail, cooking, and conversation. We'd review the day, I would be the sous-chef (chop and prepare the ingredients), so that he could work his culinary magic. While I chopped he sat and relaxed. While he cooked, it was my turn to get off my feet. We have carried this ritual over into our life with our children as well. We all gather around the island in the kitchen and talk about the events of the day and encourage the kids to get as involved in the cooking process as possible. This practice eases our transition from being out and about in the world and involved in our own activities to being peaceful and present for the evening's activities. Even if you can only incorporate this into your schedule one night a week, you will come to look forward to it and treasure the time together. Making pizza is a great project for a night like this. Get a couple of ready-made pizza crusts, a jar of sauce, and the ingredients that each member of the family likes, and let everyone make their own. Making a mess is part of the fun, so be prepared to clean up afterward. If you cook together, you can clean together as well!

Zen Homemasters

"If I can't motivate myself to do any other household chore, I can still manage to shop for groceries and cook. It helps that my husband enjoys cooking as well, so we can trade off on this duty. When we can roll up our sleeves and get to work in the kitchen, the other worries of the day seem to fade away. And then after the work, we can sit down together and enjoy the fruits of our labor."

—*Sheila Runnels*
Retail advertising manager
and mother of two
Huntsville, Alabama

KITCHEN-CLEANING CONSIDERATIONS

Here are a few additional suggestions for the fastest and most effective ways to clean your kitchen:

- Sweep your floor from the outside edges, where the most dirt and dust get pushed, toward the center, or to where your trash can is located. Sweeping thoroughly is really important, particularly when you are going to mop afterward. If you don't get up all the dirt, you will create something akin to a mud pie on the floor.

- Consider using your vacuum cleaner to ensure the floor is free from loose particles. Most vacuum cleaners have a bare-floor setting and they are great for getting up grit and crumbs that the naked eye and the average broom and dustpan can miss.

- Before you mop, use your warm soapy water to wash down cabinets and countertops that don't receive regular attention. Wipe down the outside of your oven and dishwasher with the warm water and then follow up with glass cleaner so their exteriors are clean and shiny.

- When mopping, start in the farthest corner of the room and work your way out the door. If you have to walk on the floor before it is dry, do it in a pair of clean socks. Warn family members that the floors are wet and slippery, or a major wipe-out can occur.

- Keep your disposal blades sharp and your sink sweet-smelling by putting some ice and lemon, lime, or orange peels in it and letting it grind for a minute or two. Eggshells serve a similar purpose, as grinding them will keep blades sharp, but you don't get the added benefit of the fresh citrus smell.

- I am a big fan of the Scrubbing Bubbles that "do the work so you don't have to." This product is intended for bathroom cleaning and is very effective there, but those scrubbing bubbles are phenomenal for cleaning really gooey kitchen messes, like those on your stovetop after you make a pot of spaghetti. The bubbles get busy and the mess wipes away.

- Get a spoon holder to reside by your stove and use it. Putting a pretty, ceramic spoon holder in the dishwasher is much easier than having to wipe down entire countertops.

As the heart of your home, your kitchen deserves to hold a special place in your cleaning routine. As the heart of the kitchen, *you* deserve special treatment as well. Actively seek ways to make the time you spend in the kitchen as fulfilling and rewarding as possible. Your kitchen, your loved ones, and your spirit will thank you for it.

Try This

It has been suggested here that you make every effort to walk away from all your worries while cleaning, but the truth is, sometimes a nagging problem or worry must be addressed, and often a terrific solution can occur to you during a vigorous session of cleaning. If something is really weighing on you, turn kitchen-cleaning time into problem-solving time. Is there an issue you're trying to get to the bottom of? A work situation that needs a solution? Do you need your muse to speak to you? *Now!* Pick a single topic to ponder during your next round of housekeeping. As you begin your cleaning routine, as recommended in meditation, intentionally try *not* to think about anything. Make your mind a blank slate. Most cleaning requires physical involvement but little brain power, so your mind can be free. Little ideas will begin to flow. If they are not related to your topic of choice, mentally push them aside and return to "nothingness." Your mind will eventually get the message that it's supposed to be working on a specific issue. As your body continues to work on the tasks at hand, your mind will begin to perk with ideas, inspiration, and clarity. Keep a notepad or your housekeeping journal handy to jot down ideas that have come to you while you were cleaning.

mantra for meditation on cleaning the kitchen

I am the heart of this home. Help me nourish all those who come here seeking solace.

haiku for the kitchen

foods and moods combine
hearts beating children eating
dishes call to me

zen concept

factors of enlightenment—
investigation, tranquility, and
mindfulness

cleaning koan

what is the color of clean?

THREE.

BLUE MONDAY:
LEARNING TO LOVE LAUNDRY

*W*hite is the color of purity. Red represents passion. Green is nature's color. What is the color of clean? I like to think of the color of clean as the entire color spectrum—the rainbow that you can see shimmering in a soap bubble or sparkling in a clean piece of crystal, a window, or a mirror. Or, as it has been for many generations of women beginning the labor-intensive process of doing their laundry, is blue the color of clean?

Stereotypically, it is laundry that continues to tie us to our homes and our mothers. We bring our cleaning home from college or our first apartments for our moms to do for us, the last vestige of dependence.

BLUE MONDAY

Whether the phrase "Blue Monday" referred to the intense labor required, enough to give anyone a serious case of the blues, or to the "bluing" solution used to help keep white clothes from yellowing, laundry day has, from time immemorial, been referred to as "Blue Monday."

Historically, the one thing that made the extremely difficult labor of housekeeping, and particularly laundry, tolerable, was the social interaction that came with it. Almost everyone started the lengthy process of doing laundry on Monday, and the women of the community would meet at the water well to gossip and share stories as they hung the lothes out on the line. Today's washing machines and dryers expedite the process of laundry, making it much easier to keep our families clothed and our linens fresh, but they do not feed our soul. What Zen concepts can we internalize and utilize to help us avoid "the blues"?

RESEARCH AND RINSE

I particularly like to apply the powers of *investigation* to my laundering tasks. What stains need to be treated? What are the instructions for washing this particular article of clothing? What detergents, temperature, and spin cycle should be used from load to load?

The first mystery that must be investigated on laundry day is "Where are all the clothes?!" It seems that laundry piles up at various locations all over the house—on bathroom floors, in hampers, just outside the closet. It's difficult to even know what you have to tackle unless you can see it. Try devoting two days a week to laundry, whatever days work for you. On the appointed days, get all the dirty clothes to one place and sort them into piles by color or type of item. For example, a lot of towels can be washed together regardless of color. Towels and sweat clothes or fleece should always be washed separately from other clothing. The fuzz from them is like a magnet to your favorite work and dress clothes. *Everything* red or dark pink should be in a load together. Who hasn't wound up with pink underwear because of a stray red sock or T-shirt? Be vigilant in keeping reds and pinks to themselves!

If your laundry room is big enough to serve as your appointed separation station, great. It's been my experience, however, that most laundry rooms are barely big enough to hold the washer and dryer, let alone sort the clothes. So on laundry day, my kitchen becomes the halfway house for piles of dirty clothes. Just dedicate a place for sorting the clothes that is close to your washer and dryer and will not be a high traffic area on laundry day.

Once laundry is sorted by color and type, make sure that you are not neglecting clothes with special needs. Make a pile for things that need to be hand-washed or taken to the dry cleaner. I usually have another pile for clothes that are clean but somehow made it back into the hampers with the other dirties. Pretreat any stains. One of the greatest innovations for modern-day laundry is the pen that you can carry with you to pretreat or eliminate stains as soon as they happen. Get several and keep one in your purse, if you're married send one with your spouse, and if you have children that are old enough to understand the concept, stick one in their back pack. The most difficult part of laundry is removing stains that are already set into clothes. If you miss a stain and it makes it through the entire washing and drying cycle, it is almost impossible to remove. If stains receive immediate treatment or are at least treated before they get into the washing machine, the clothing can usually be salvaged.

A few other prewashing preparation tips to make laundry day easier on you and your clothes:

- Fasten all fasteners (buttons, zippers, hooks, snaps, etc.). This will help maintain the shape of the clothing and keep these items from snagging others.
- Turn pockets inside out prior to washing to eliminate accumulated grime and grit (and find the change that's hiding there).
- Turn brightly colored and patterned clothes inside out so they will wear less quickly.

After you have completed your preparation, dive into the first pile and keep a load of clothes rotating from the washer to the dryer to your chosen place for folding and ironing until all the piles are gone.

The knobs and dials on your washing machine and dryer are there for a reason. Use them! If you follow the written instructions present on almost every piece of clothing, your clothes will last longer, look better, and often cause less work for you. Many of your clothes will fare better if you take them directly out of the washer and hang them to dry. The heat and hostility that clothes are subjected to in the dryer will wear them out more quickly. Another benefit for you is that many items will not require ironing if you hang them to dry. You might even consider putting up an old-fashioned clothesline in your backyard and hanging some things out to line dry. A lot of the fragrance-filled laundry products on the market today strive to mimic that "fresh from the clothesline" smell. Why not just hang it on the clothesline in the first place! Hang lights and whites in the sun and dark-colored items in the shade.

Whatever choices you make in the maintenance of your laundry, just don't stop the process until everything is cleaned and dried if at all possible. There is no other household chore that can hang over your head or feel like more of a constant nagging duty than laundry. If you see it through to completion two days a week, you will, at last, feel some freedom from it!

Living One with Nature

Adding half a cup of distilled white vinegar to the final rinse cycle of your laundry instead of liquid fabric softener will:

- Soften clothes
- Be less irritating to family members with sensitive skin
- Break down laundry detergent more effectively, making it less harmful to the environment after its use
- Reduce static cling
- Minimize lint buildup
- Help keep pet and human hair from clinging to the clothes

INSIDE OUT

Why do we fold our clothes? For neatness certainly, and to turn shirts, socks, and underwear right side out. But isn't it really to make big things fit into small spaces? Our spirituality is something big that many of us reserve for Sunday services or for times of trouble, folding it away to fit into a small space at other times. Zen allows you to integrate your spirituality into everything you do, large or small.

Another great thing about the chore of folding clothes is that it's one of the few chores that is portable. You can move a pile of clothes that need folding anywhere in the house. Zen is portable as well. Take it with you. It will always serve you well.

As you fold clothes, contemplate the *tranquility* factor of enlightenment. Folding clothes can be quiet and soothing. Take your clothes out of the dryer and fold them while they are still warm. Let that warmth radiate and calm you from the outside in. Feel the different fabric textures between your fingers. Look at the colors, consider the shapes and sizes, and reflect on your feelings about the person that wears those clothes. Every time I pick up a pair of tiny socks, it brings a smile to my face. If I'm in the right frame of mind and living my Zen, every piece of clothing I fold reminds me of the wearer and the activity he or she most recently enjoyed while wearing it. It's a miniature trip down memory lane and infuses the folding with meaning.

While you're folding, have a stack of hangers close by (collecting empty hangers from around the house is a great chore for kids).

Seeds of Rapture

Roll clothes instead of folding to reduce wrinkles and minimize the space needed for storage. For example, T-shirts or shorts that are folded, stacked, and placed in drawers can come out looking like origami (the Japanese art of paper folding) when you are ready to wear them. Instead, fold them in half lengthwise and then roll them from top to bottom. This is also a great tip to try when traveling. Roll all items and line them up in your suitcases. You will be able to pack more into a smaller space and your clothes will look much better when you arrive at your destination.

It is very frustrating to be enjoying the peaceful process of folding clothes and having to disturb it on a quest for a hanger. Get the clothes hung and into their respective closets and the folded clothes put away—immediately. Take a deep breath and enjoy the sense of accomplishment.

STEAMING ALONG

Ironing is very symbolic. Flattening out the wrinkles in our clothes is like smoothing out the rough edges of our lives. With all the new materials that are available, not to mention our use of dry cleaners,

Living One with Nature

Homemade dryer sheets are as simple as combining one part liquid fabric softener with two parts water and spraying a dry, clean washcloth with the mixture. This freshens your laundry, minimizes static, and there are no dryer sheets stuck to your clothes or freshening a landfill!

many of us rarely even turn on an iron. I, however, intentionally keep my husband's dress shirts at home to be laundered. I'd love to say that it's a protest against the chemicals that dry cleaners use, but it's actually that I just really enjoy ironing. The seeds of my enjoyment of ironing were sown during childhood.

When I was on the verge of young womanhood, about to become a teenager, my mother and I had our first "showdown" of me expressing my independence. As far back as I can remember she wouldn't allow me to buy clothes that were 100 percent cotton because they were too difficult to iron and she did all the ironing. Hindsight being twenty-twenty I can now look back and see her point, but at the time I felt that it was a ridiculous line to draw in the sand. What was the big deal? On this particular occasion we were out shopping for a dress for me to wear to a friend's bar mitzvah, the Jewish rite of passage for young men turning thirteen. I fell in love with a dress, the most beautiful dress I had ever seen, that was a beautiful deep pink, almost purple, with pleats and ruffles in all the right places, a unique combination of femininity and classic style that I thought was absolutely perfect for me and the occasion. It was summertime and the dress would set off my tan and sun-highlighted hair to perfection. I had to have it. My mother said absolutely not. Not only was the dress 100 percent cotton, but it was a lightweight Indian cotton that would wrinkle if you looked at it wrong; the detail that made it so beautiful and unique would make it a nightmare to iron, and the deep shade of pink would ensure that it would bleed on everything it came into contact with, she explained.

I begged, I pleaded, and ultimately promised on all that my twelve-year-old self held dear that I would care for the dress myself. Not only would I wash it (always by itself or with "like colors"), but I would iron it as well. I got the dress. I did look stunning in it. And it was a *horror* to iron. But on that day, I experienced my own rite of passage. I made the decision that I would and could care for something if I really loved it. It is an experience that has stayed with me and I still ponder occasionally as I smooth out the rough edges of my clothes and the clothes of my family.

Where folding clothes takes big things and makes them smaller, ironing is based on attention to detail—it forces us to focus on the small. The small space between buttons on a shirt front or the smoothing of the epaulets (shoulder seams), make all the difference between a well-pressed garment and looking like you just rolled out of bed. The nature of ironing makes it a wonderful opportunity for practicing your *kinhin*—walking meditation. You are accomplishing a necessary task, but you are free to be quiet and

Living One with Nature

Make your own spray starch without the aerosol emissions and packaging waste by combining one tablespoon of cornstarch with two cups of water and stirring until the cornstarch is dissolved. Put the mixture in a spray bottle and mist it onto clothes while ironing. Shake the bottle thoroughly before each use.

mindful as you execute the necessary maneuvers. You are dealing with heat, steam, and a heavy appliance, which require your complete awareness. An untended ironing board could spell disaster if a hot, heavy iron fell on the floor or onto the head of someone playing beneath it. But as long as safety considerations are kept in mind, you are relatively free to focus your attention inward and spend a few restorative and meditative moments preparing the clothes of the ones you love.

Buddha Says . . .
"Let us rise and be thankful, for if we didn't learn a lot today, at least we learned a little, and if we didn't learn a little, at least we didn't get sick, and if we got sick, at least we didn't die; so let us be thankful."

As with your washer and dryer, the controls on your iron are also there for a reason. If you avoid ironing because you don't like the way it spits and leaves spots on your clothes, you are doing something wrong. Today's irons are far more complicated than the cast iron flatirons our foremothers rotated on and off a hot stovetop, but they are still relatively straightforward. A spitting, spotting iron is either on the wrong setting or you have used water to fill it for steam that is too rich in mineral content. Distilled water is best for most irons and you should keep a bottle of it handy in your laundry room for the purpose of filling your iron. It is also important to empty the iron of water after each use. The internal parts can rust and the rust can cause stains on your clothing that are difficult to remove.

"You can't get spoiled if you do your own ironing."

—*Meryl Streep*

Additional ironing tips:

- Iron clothes inside-out to minimize a shiny appearance to the fabric.
- Iron the back of clothes first and move to the front so that the front of garments will be most attractive and wrinkle free.
- Iron the clothes that require the coolest setting first and work your way up to the clothes that require the hottest setting.
- If your iron isn't producing enough steam, use a Q-tip to clean the steam vents on the bottom plate.
- If your iron becomes clogged with mineral deposits and starts spewing gunky buildup onto your clothes, put ⅓ of a cup of vinegar and ⅓ of a cup of water into the steam reservoir, allowing it to steam for a few minutes. Rinse it thoroughly with clear water before using it again.

Ironing is a task that requires a great deal of preparation and encourages you to stay grounded in reality. Getting your iron out and filling it, putting up your ironing board, gathering hangers, and

Zen Homemasters

"I have tried to find ways to make things have a higher meaning or purpose. Instead of hating ironing school uniforms every morning, I try to take that time to pray over my daughter's day and what she will be doing in those clothes. It takes the emphasis off the ironing and puts it on something else."

—*Darcie Conrad*
Mother of two, community volunteer
Hattiesburg, Mississippi

all the work that goes into ironing preparation is not something you want to have to do on a daily basis. It is far more effective to collect ironing from your multiple cycles of laundry and complete it all at one time, preferably once a week. I use ironing as therapy for my Sunday afternoon blues.

Viktor Frankl, noted psychologist and author of the classic book *Man's Search for Meaning*, found that these Sunday afternoon blues are very common and called the condition "Sunday neurosis." Frankl stated that this condition reveals the presence of an existential vacuum. He theorized that we are so busy during the week that we don't have time to think about our lives and it is only when things slow down a bit, for most people on a Sunday afternoon, that we realize there is a void in our lives, an empty place that needs to be filled with something meaningful. By setting up the ironing board on a Sunday afternoon and working methodically through all the ironing for the week ahead, I make this down time purposeful. I pave the way for more peaceful mornings during the week, setting myself up for success. Sunday afternoons are also a good time for contemplation, and ironing is one of the most contemplative pastimes I know. I can reflect on the sermon from church that morning, plan for the week ahead, or simply use all I've learned about meditation to listen to the sound of my breath, the sound of the steam as it pulses from the iron, and observe the way the rough edges of a piece of clothing are smoothed by the work of my hand. Now instead of

Buddha Says . . .
"He is able who thinks he is able."

dreading Sunday afternoons, I welcome the opportunity I find not only to prepare my family, but to calm my mind as well. As you are devising and revising your housekeeping system, you may look for a place and time in your schedule where your mind and spirit are usually in need of rejuvenation and consider if that would be a good time to schedule the week's necessary ironing. Perhaps you too can use ironing to smooth the rough edges of your life.

TRY THIS

Give your laundry room a makeover. Laundry rooms are almost always incredibly small spaces in which to try to tackle incredibly large jobs. Take a long, hard look at the space and see how you can utilize it more effectively. What is in the laundry room cabinets that can be moved to another location to free up valuable space? Make a trip to Target or The Container Store and look at the products available to organize the space. Do you have a place to hang clothes to dry as they come out of the washing machine? Do you have a place to hang clothes as you pull them from the dryer? Are your stain pretreaters, laundry soap, and dryer sheets within easy reach? Purchase a small trash can for your laundry room for lint from the dryer's filter, used dryer sheets, and junk pulled from people's pockets. Also purchase a cute container or piggy bank to keep the loose change that always appears as you do the laundry. Save this money and when you have collected enough, treat yourself to something frivolous. Consider it payment for a job well done! If you want to be really nice about it, use the money to take your family out to dinner, but I like to consider it my own personal fun money.

mantra for meditation on laundry

Bless all those who wear these clothes, dry themselves in these towels, and sleep on these sheets. Let them go into the world wrapped in warmth, comfort, and love.

haiku for blue monday

swirling and spinning
water washes away dirt
i am still and strong

FOUR.

BUDDHA IN THE BATHROOM

*T*ry to describe "clean." I find myself using words like *fresh, crisp, citrusy,* or *shiny.* There is, of course, the sound of something that is "squeaky clean," but for the most part, the descriptors we use when defining the concept of cleanliness are about sights or smells. What does clean really *sound* like and where can we go in our homes to best hear the sound of clean?

I think clean can best be heard as quiet and that clean is loudest in the bathroom. The sound of clean is about a sense of peacefulness, and with a base of cleanliness, it is fun and rewarding to create a sanctuary in your bathrooms that will allow you to go there for refuge from the storms of life.

THE JOKE'S ON ME

Before I had children, bathroom time was the ultimate in private time, and long, luxurious baths were an almost daily indulgence. Friends with children would lament that the only time they got to be alone was when they went to the bathroom, and even then, it wouldn't be long before little hands were pounding on the door and the kids were screaming at the top of their lungs about a crisis that could only be resolved by Mom. I thought they were joking! They were not. Thus, keeping bathrooms clean takes on even greater significance: You've got to clean, kill germs, and disinfect for health reasons, and you also need to reserve one bathroom in the house that can be *your* escape.

To effectively address this multiplicity of purpose in keeping your bathrooms clean, you can enlist another factor of enlightenment: *concentration*.

Most homes didn't even have indoor plumbing until around the turn of the century, so cleaning bathrooms is a relatively recent addition to the role of a homemaker. And yet, the vast majority of cleaning products found at stores are for cleaning the bathroom. Additionally, a multi-million-dollar industry has sprung up around aromatherapy bath products, specialized soaps, lotions, and potions. So others have also realized the dual nature necessary to create a clean and comforting bathroom. How do we accomplish this feat?

New products are appearing on the market faster than today's busy woman can keep up with them. The first thing you can do away with is the bacteria-ridden toilet brush that lurks in the corner of your bathroom. The disposable pads and brushes pretreated with cleansers are just as effective, if not more effective, than the toilet brushes of old. It's hard to believe somebody didn't come up with that concept sooner.

Another recent addition to the bathroom-cleaning marketplace is the spray that you apply after each use of the shower to minimize the buildup of soap scum and virtually eliminate the scrubbing of shower doors. I don't think they've come up with a better way to clean the bathtub than on your hands and knees with a sponge and some mildly abrasive cleanser, but if you tackle that task on a weekly basis, the time and work invested should be minimal.

Bathroom floors remain a challenge. Cracks, crevices, the dead space behind toilets—all are hard to reach and harbingers of really nasty buildups. Full utilization of disposable mops is your best tool for tackling these areas. You do not want to expose a mop that you will use in other areas of your house to the grime of bathrooms. Purchase one with a swiveling head and a pad or sheet that can be thrown away after each use, and those hard to reach places won't seem nearly so challenging.

Living One with Nature

Create your own "soft scrub" by combining half a cup of baking soda with enough vegetable-based liquid soap to make a paste. If you are a fan of fragrance, add a few drops of essential oils (naturally occuring aromatic oils that are extracted from plant sources), scrub, and rinse. This is good for use on your bathroom countertops and tubs.

Seeds of Rapture

The bathroom is the place where you care for your face, hair, and body. It should be treated as a sacred space. More tips for totally clean bathrooms:

- Sprinkle baking soda on tough stains in the tub, shower, or on bathroom cabinets. Let it sit and then scrub with a sponge.
- Dip a sponge in white vinegar and clean glass shower doors with it.
- You can also use vinegar to clean mirrors. Sheets of newspaper dipped in vinegar won't leave lint or streaks on your mirrors. After wiping the mirror with the vinegar, dry it with another sheet of newspaper.
- A cup of liquid fabric softener diluted in a quart of warm water will help clean soap scum from tubs and showers.
- Use a dry cloth to apply a layer of furniture polish to tile walls to prevent buildup and water spots.

And kids bathrooms? Especially if you have boys and/or are trying to potty train, cleaning the bathrooms used by your children can seem as dangerous as a trip to a biohazardous dumping ground. Invest in several pairs of rubber gloves. I like to stock up on the pink ones that are for sale during the month of October with a portion of the proceeds going to breast cancer research. With a pair of rubber gloves on, you can face almost anything! Once you have done the scrubbing, be sure to spray your bathrooms with Lysol or some other type of antibacterial spray. Just because the bathroom looks clean, there can still be germs that may have survived the attack of a round of scrubbing (and it no longer has to smell so medicinal: Lysol has come out with a line of really nice-smelling sprays).

Once the dirty work of cleaning your bathrooms has been dealt with, it is time to focus on the fun of creating a quiet, peaceful oasis. I have just recently recovered from a teeny, tiny drip inside the wall that turned into $7,000 worth of repairs needed to get my master bathroom back to working condition. My first priority? A large, deep, whirlpool bathtub. We had been bathing in a tub that most closely resembled a roasting pan, and when I knew my bathroom was going to have to undergo a major overhaul, I was determined to create a place that was beautiful, nurturing, and functional. I chose to use colors that reflected those in nature for the paint and tile floors. Greens, oranges, chocolate browns. Rich colors that speak to me of warmth and growth. We made a minimal investment in candles and aromatherapy bath oils and purchased big, fluffy bath sheets. Last, we hung a two-pronged hook on the back of the door and on each hook hung a fat, snuggly bathrobe, one for me and one for my husband. These are simple and inexpensive upgrades that transform your bathroom from simple utilitarianism into a private escape where you can explore your senses and renew your spirit.

Buddha Says . . .

"On life's journey faith is nourishment, virtuous deeds are a shelter, wisdom is the light by day and right mindfulness is the protection by night. If a man lives a pure life, nothing can destroy him."

Lucky for us, the bathroom was completed and ready for use on Friday, just in time for date night. We grilled steaks and played in the backyard with the kids. The outdoor activity, the big meal, and a lavender-scented bubble bath for the children guaranteed (we thought) that they would get to bed early and sleep soundly, allowing us to test out our newly revamped oasis. Aromatherapy oil with the enticing title "Unwind" had been poured in the bathtub. The candles were lit. The wine was poured. My husband was submerged in the steamy water and had hit "start" on the massaging bubbles of the Jacuzzi and beckoned me to join him. I piled my hair on top of my head and clipped it, slid my clothes off seductively, and as the big toe on my right foot touched the water. . . .

Bang! Bang! Bang!

"Mommy! I need to poo poo!" shrieked my three-year-old daughter. The spell was broken as surely as it was when the clock struck midnight on Cinderella. When you are a parent, it is more likely than not those moments of peace and tranquility will be interrupted. That doesn't mean you shouldn't try to take them – or *make* them! Our next attempt at a romantic rendezvous in the Jacuzzi went off without a hitch, and it was all the more meaningful because of the prior interruption. Don't give up! Put all the pieces of the puzzle in place that you can. When the moment

Zen Homemasters

"Sometimes, the only way I can get through cleaning the bathroom is to imagine the hot bubble bath that is waiting for me when it is all over. While I am scrubbing the toilet, my mind is up to my neck in lavender-scented bath bubbles."

—*Lisa Ruggles*
Entrepreneur and mother of one
Albuquerque, New Mexico

presents itself, you can shut out the world, either alone or together, and listen for the sound of clean.

I admit, as eager as I was to fully embrace Zen concepts, and as excited as I was about creating my own oasis, looking for enlightenment in the scrubbing of a toilet was still a challenge. As always, I turned to my beloved books for inspiration, and scanning the bookshelves I rediscovered a gem that provided me not only another answer to the "What is the sound of clean?" koan but also a shortcut to enlightenment. I came across a book my mother gave me for college graduation, *All I Really Needed to Know I Learned in Kindergarten*, by Robert Fulghum. It is a collection of short essays, all of which are a beautiful blend of humor and inspiration.

Fulghum's work is well known, particularly his "kindergarten" essay, but his work took on personal significance to my family. Fulghum is

Buddha Says . . .

"All that we are is the result of what we have thought. The mind is everything. What we think we become."

an ordained Unitarian minister and came to give a lecture at my parent's Unitarian church in Austin several years ago. As all the attendees chatted over coffee after the lecture, Mr. Fulghum said he needed a ride back to his hotel. No limos or car service for this down-to-earth man! My parents were more than happy to oblige, and so it was that my mom and dad had the opportunity to spend some one-on-one time with this well-known thinker, writer, and modern-day philosopher. My mom says he was one of the kindest people she had ever met. My parents were thrilled just to have the opportunity to visit with him and perform a needed act of kindness. They certainly expected no payment of any kind. But before he got out of their car at his hotel, Mr. Fulghum pulled out a copy of the kindergarten book and autographed it. It is that copy that now graces my shelves.

Fulghum's kindergarten concepts are profound in their simplicity (like Zen!), and several relate to cleaning! Clear, concise, and classic advice like "put things back where you found them," "clean up your own mess," "wash your hands before you eat," and the one simple word that shed light on my search for enlightenment in cleaning the bathroom: "Flush!"

Flush is a powerful word, an idea that brings to mind both a vivid mental picture of water swirling down the pipes and that unmistakable whooshing sound with which we are all familiar. Perhaps *flush* should become our bathroom cleaning mantra—the word we repeat over and over to remind us why we are there.

As you go about cleaning your bathrooms, try making it an exercise in eliminating bad feelings or negative thoughts. As you scrub the toilet or cleanse the bathtub, wipe down the fixtures, and disinfect the surfaces around your sinks, go ahead and let yourself contemplate problems or negative thoughts. Address issues that are troubling you. Feel them fully and take out your frustrations as you clean. If you are mad at your boss or frustrated with your spouse, scrub that sink with far greater force. The germs in your bathroom won't stand a fighting chance with you applying your full fury. When you've scoured every surface

Living One with Nature

Create your own "Green" drain cleaner.
- Pour half a cup of baking soda down a clogged drain.
- Pour half a cup of vinegar on top.
- Let it bubble and fizz for a few minutes, then add hot water to flush.

You can also do this routine on a regular basis as preventative maintenance to keep drains from clogging.

and contemplated every issue that is causing you angst, turn on the water and rinse them down the drain. Last but not least, flush. Walk away from your bathroom-cleaning with a lighter heart and a clearer head, with the knowledge that there is no problem you can't handle.

And what of Fulghum's shortcut to enlightenment? The essay includes a phrase that truly embodies the "live in the moment and appreciate each one fully" way to live Zen. It states: "Live a balanced life. Learn some and think some and draw and paint and sing and dance and play and work every day some."

Living One with Nature

- Put undiluted vinegar in your toilet bowl to eliminate rings.
- Rub a lemon or use the juice of a lemon to treat soap scum or hard-water deposits in your bathtub or on shower doors.
- Use baking soda anywhere you would use an abrasive store-bought cleaner. Baking soda is far less abrasive than its store-bought counterparts and not nearly as likely to leave scratches. Plus, it is nontoxic.

TRY THIS

Once you've found your favorite bathroom-cleaning tools and products, put together a set for each bathroom in your house and leave them there. Even cleaning the bathroom can seem relatively quick and painless if you have everything you need at your fingertips. If you have to spend time traipsing around the house collecting supplies, the moment of opportunity and motivation may pass and the "I'll do it later" syndrome will snuff out your best intentions. Stock up on rubber gloves at the dollar store and leave a pair with each set of bathroom-cleaning supplies. You'll be less apt to be slowed down worrying about the icky factor of bathroom grime if you protect your hands with rubber gloves.

mantra for meditating when cleaning the bathroom

The buddha says do no harm,
but that does not apply to killing
germs. Guide me in making this
bathroom clean so that
the bodies, minds, and spirits of
those who use it can flourish.

haiku to a clean bathroom

flush away worries
listening for quiet sounds
send cares down the drain

FIVE.

ROOTS AND WINGS: CLEANING THE FLOORS

*D*o you remember padding down the hallway of your home at 4 A.M. to nurse your first child? Or pacing the floors waiting for a tardy teenager to arrive home? Have you ever danced in the kitchen with the man you love? What symbolic footprints have been left on your floors as you went about both the large and small moments of your life? It is my belief that everywhere we go and everything we do leaves a mark on those people and places we encounter. Where do we leave more of these "footprints" than in our homes?

The energy required for sweeping, mopping, and vacuuming your floors is comparable to the energy you have to invest in laying the groundwork for any worthwhile work. As that well-known saying goes, all parents want to give their children roots and wings.

The floors are the literal roots of your home. Their maintenance can give wings to all who walk there.

COUNTRY CLUBBER

When my first child was a mere six weeks old, we moved from Louisiana to Pennsylvania. My husband had taken a job with a newspaper in Trenton, New Jersey, and we elected to live just across the Delaware River in Pennsylvania. The cost of living in that region was astronomical, unlike anything we Southerners had ever encountered. This greatly complicated the task of looking for a home. In Louisiana, we had left behind a big beautiful home on the lake, with an in-ground swimming pool and five acres of land. In our new locale, homes like that were reserved for millionaires and we weren't in that ballpark. We settled on a personality-filled place in a charming older neighborhood. It was small but pretty with lots of landscaping and "mature" trees, French doors leading to the backyard, an upstairs loft, and a sun-filled back bedroom that would make a beautiful nursery.

We were just looking for a decent house that we could afford. Little did we know we were buying a piece of history. We had purchased a house that had initially been built in the fifties, in the second phase of the suburban dream known as Levittown.

As GI's began returning home after World War II and the babies of the baby-boom generation began to be born, forward-thinking New York developer Abraham Levitt, along with his two sons William and Alfred, announced that they would build 2,000 low-cost homes and make them available for veterans to rent. Levitt realized that by building small affordable homes, he could provide those veterans with the American Dream, and get rich beyond his wildest dreams in the process. Levittown, New York, built on Long Island, was more successful than the Levitts could have hoped. They announced plans to build 4,000 more rental homes and once those were taken, decided building homes for purchase and developing communities around those homes would be the next step in their plan. Using precut and prefabricated materials and a style of assembly that most closely imitated a production line, Levitt & Sons got to the point where they could construct 30 homes a day, ultimately building over 17,000 by the start of the 1950s, and earning themselves

Buddha Says . . .

"The way is not in the sky. The way is in the heart."

the title of creator of the modern American suburb. The New York Levittown was so successful that they developed a second community in Bucks County, north of Philadelphia, Pennsylvania. What made Pennsylvania's Levittown unique was that it was the first truly planned community, with only six available floor plans (ours was a Country Clubber), roads constructed to minimize speeding, space included for schools, churches, parks, pools, and even a shopping center.

The footprints that history had left on that house and that neighborhood were profound. In fact, the entire area was awash in history. We lived about five miles from the community of

Washington's Crossing, so named because it was the site where George Washington and his troops camped out before their Christmas Day journey across the Delaware River. The scene is forever etched in our collective memory by the famous painting by Emanuel Leutze that shows Washington standing proudly in the bow of his boat. It was that crossing that changed the course of our country's history, giving the beleaguered troops that were about to quit the fight a boost of confidence and a renewed faith in their leader. They might indeed have a fighting chance to win this war and gain independence from England.

We spent many weekends in the Center City district of Philadelphia, walking around Independence Hall in the footsteps of patriots such as Thomas Jefferson and Benjamin Franklin, visiting the house where Betsy Ross first sewed an American flag, and marveling at the size of the crack in the Liberty Bell. The footprints that have been laid in our homes are not of this historical magnitude, and yet, they are even more important to us as we journey toward enlightenment. They are the footprints that have created our own personal histories and will leave our future legacy.

As you rid your home of the real footprints left there through sweeping, mopping, and vacuuming your floors, consider the footprints you have left behind and the footprints you hope to leave in the future. Floor maintenance is one of the most physically demanding of household chores, so let us ponder the factor of enlightenment, *energy*, as we look for meaning in their cleaning.

THE KARMA OF CLEANING YOUR CARPET

When you fall in love, someone *sweeps* you off your feet. When you win every game of a series, you make a clean *sweep*. You can be *swept* away on a wave of emotion. Or if you want to keep a secret, you can *sweep* something under the rug. Why is sweeping such a powerful concept? It is the first line in our defense against dirt. If we don't sweep, we can't continue on to the next steps of floor maintenance. It is us against dirt, and with a broom on our side, we can almost always emerge victorious. It is also a quick spruce-up for any hard floor surface in your home.

There are more types of brooms available than you could possibly imagine. The most important differences for your average keeper of the home are whether the broom's bristles are synthetic or natural fibers and whether the head of the broom is straight-edged or angled. They all have pros and cons, but primarily it is a matter of choice. For most of our cleaning needs, a synthetic broom with an angled head is great. The angle allows you to get into corners and underneath hard-to-reach places. For smooth floors, synthetic fibers are adequately sturdy to do the job. A new decorating trend in flooring today is toward stained concrete floors. If you have floors with more texture like that or are looking for a broom for outside chores, you will probably want to go with a heavier-duty natural fiber product. Pick out the right dustpan for your needs and you are on your way. A dustpan isn't a place to save money. In this case it pays to get a sturdy, high-quality dustpan, or you will find you've left behind more dirt than you picked up. I also like the sets of broom and dustpan that snap together. You always have them both at hand for any given job. When you are storing your brooms, hang them either upside down (with bristles up) or at least where they are not touching the floor. Broom bristles are easily bent and make the broom much less effective. Many companies that produce cleaning products have developed their own version of the Swiffer Sweeper, the sweeping tool that has replaceable pads you just throw away after use. These have their place for picking up dust, hair, and the like and are great for picking up the dust that settles behind cabinets and pieces of furniture on a hardwood floor, but for a truly thorough sweeping, nothing beats a good old-fashioned broom and dustpan.

Once you have completed your sweeping, the next step in your floor maintenance process is mopping. Sweeping and mopping have recently become even more important and time-consuming jobs around the house as our ideas about interior decorating have evolved. In addition to the stained concrete flooring mentioned previously, many houses now have hardwood floors, tiles, or laminates that *look* like hardwood or tile in addition to the tried-and-true linoleum. When it comes to mopping, you need to be very aware of what type of material your floors are made of and what the directions are for its care. Each type of flooring requires specific products and processes to keep them looking their best.

Concrete Floors

If you are cleaning an unfinished concrete floor (the surface in the vast majority of garages for example), you will need to sweep it thoroughly and use a pretty heavy-duty all-purpose cleaner. This surface is extremely porous and will pick up stains from everything, so in addition to your high-powered cleaner you will also have to use a bit of elbow grease. Fortunately, a concrete floor that is inside our home will almost always be sealed and is therefore very low maintenance. Just a quick wet mopping with warm water and a mild cleaning solution will keep it looking great. This type of floor gives you immense versatility in color and pattern, limited only by your imagination, but they are cold and they are hard. Soften surfaces, both literally and visually, with area rugs.

Hardwood Flooring

The warmth, richness, and beauty of hardwood floors make them extremely desirable. The difficulty of caring for them and maintaining that beauty can minimize their appeal. There was a time when the home of my dreams that I envisioned in my mind's eye had all wood floors. Then I actually lived in a home with hardwood floors and have avoided them ever since. If you are looking at buying a new home or redoing your floors, I wouldn't recommend hardwood floors if you have small children or animals. Puppy and kitty toenails, children's toys, and the way they play make scratches and gouges in the surface almost an inevitability. Consider saving hardwoods for your home when the kids are a bit older. Or look into a vinyl or linoleum floor that is made to look like wood. There are some really beautiful "imitation" wood floors that look so good you can hardly tell the difference.

If you truly have your heart set on wood floors (or already have them), know the procedure for maintenance of them, and are willing to do the work needed to keep them looking their best, they are a beautiful surface on which to live your life.

- For hardwood floors, wet mopping with soap and water is a big no-no!
- Wipe up any spills immediately with a dry cloth.
- Look for a quality one-step wood cleaner or polish and rub one small section at a time with a cloth or sponge, going with the grain of the wood.
- When I had wood floors, I *loved* the Swiffer Sweeper for quick pickups of dust.

Ceramic Tile

Tile floors have long been popular in kitchens and bathrooms, but they are now becoming far more commonplace throughout living areas as well. Their care is simple and straightforward. Just wet mop with warm water and an all-purpose cleaner and air-dry or dry with a soft cloth if you want to prevent streaking. If you want your tiles to shine, you can polish the floor (as well as tile kitchen countertops) with car wax and buff them.

Marble

Unless your home has a ballroom, the main place you will find marble flooring is in an entryway or perhaps a master

Seeds of Rapture

Chances are you will have a variety of materials that make up the floors of your home, so you will have to use a combination of cleaning methods. Don't get overwhelmed by the multitude of floor-cleaning products available. Read the labels to determine the best product for your type of flooring and follow the instructions to the letter. Your floors will soon reflect the beauty that you are finding in your heart and in your home as you pursue peaceful housekeeping practices through Zen.

bathroom. You can mop marble floors with straight water or with an all-purpose cleaner and they will look great. For an extra shiny marble floor, a coat of liquid wax will do the trick, but the buildup will need to be stripped annually and reapplied.

Vinyl and Linoleum

These tried-and-true flooring staples have withstood the test of time and the influx of new flooring materials and are very common. This is due in large part to the ease with which they can be cleaned. Wipe up spills with a damp sponge and wet mop with an all-purpose cleaner and warm water. Want to add extra shine? Add a cup of vinegar to warm water and mop again. Do not use hot water on vinyl or linoleum, as it can soften the surface and make it more susceptible to damage.

For a basic wet mopping:

● Pick up all your area rugs, take them outside, shake out any accumulated dust or dirt, and put them aside.

- You can use a bucket or a sink for your mop water, but the sink is really preferable because you have easy access to both your soapy water and clear water to rinse with.
- Get your mop well saturated with liquid and then wring it out.
- Develop a pattern and stick to it so you can make sure to get the entire floor clean.
- Rinse your mop regularly with clear water and resaturate and wring it in your cleaning solution.
- Let the floor and your mop dry thoroughly after rinsing your mop in clear water for a last time.

The type of floor you have and your personal preference will dictate the type of mop you use. I am partial to an old-fashioned string mop, but there are definitely advantages to sponge mops, mops with self-wringing action, and more. Swiffer struck again with the Swiffer WetJet, and these tools can indeed make quick cleanups much easier. A deep cleaning is best done with a traditional mop, but the WetJet and other products like it work great for day-to-day maintenance.

THE VACUUM CLEANER: IT'S NOT JUST FOR FLOORS ANYMORE

Almost all home interiors used to have as a prerequisite wall-to-wall carpeting (and *shag* carpeting at that!). Our carpets are now more likely to be area rugs or runners and thus our floor maintenance is much more important. If we do have carpet in large spaces, it is likely to be a Berber or some other type of low-maintenance material. Thus our vacuum cleaners may not be called upon with the regularity they were in bygone days—unless we learn to use this underutilized tool to its full advantage. In that case, the vacuum cleaner can be a direct link to enlightenment. Use it to dust, clean blinds and window-sills, suck cobwebs out of corners, clean ceiling fans, decrud vents, and you can even use it on your carpets! If you ignore the attachments that came with your vacuum cleaner, you are missing a great opportunity to make many cleaning jobs around your home easier. If you can't figure it out on your own (and usually switching over to use those tools requires at least switching a setting or two and making sure the attachments are installed correctly), refer back to your owner's manual or look up the vacuum's make and model online. The time and effort put into a little research will be well worth it as you suck corners clean and remove the muck under couch cushions with a minimum of trouble.

Living One with Nature

Baking soda is a natural deodorizer. Why do you think you've been putting a box in the back of your refrigerator all these years? Instead of sprinkling highly fragranced deodorizers on your carpet, sprinkle baking soda liberally and then vacuum.

As for basic vacuuming, just make sure you've looked closely at the space you are about to vacuum and picked up items like loose change, bobby pins, and paper clips. Clean out the filter or change bags regularly and replace the belts regularly as well. Sprinkle a lightly fragranced deodorizer over your carpet and then begin. Vacuums work more effectively if you use long, slow strokes (it's a lot like mowing the lawn in that respect) and overlap a little on each stroke so you don't miss anything. It's a pain, but it is worth it to go ahead and move whatever furniture you can and vacuum underneath. Pop up recliner footrests and vacuum under them. Move step stools and end tables. Remember the area and throw rugs and runners that we moved from our floors while we mopped? After you shake them outside, bring them in and run the vacuum cleaner over them as well. Just be careful about getting too close to the edges, as they can easily get sucked into the vacuum cleaner and ruin the rug as well as the cleaner.

Every square inch of your home has flooring of some type. Maintaining the floors is a big job but one that is critical in your pursuit of good housekeeping karma. It is the ground level, literally and figuratively, of everything

Zen Homemasters

"My husband doesn't do much in the way of cleaning around the house, but when he does, the job he likes best is sweeping and mopping the floors. I don't know if it's because it reminds him of mowing the yard or what, but when we have company coming over, I give him a broom and a mop and he gets to it. The chore he will *never* help with? Cleaning the bathroom!"

—*Stacie Conner*
Homemaker and mother of two
Newtown, Pennsylvania

Seeds of Rapture

Vacuuming spruces up your house more quickly than almost any other task. You get the visual clues of the fluffed-up carpet and a fresh smell from sucking out the accumulated dust and dirt.

that takes place in your home. It is a joy to feel comfortable knowing you can roll around on the floor wrestling with your kids, or sit on the floor in front of the fireplace and sip a glass of wine, either alone or with your beloved. Investing the time and energy into preparing this foundation for living will allow those that inhabit your home to have a firm foundation as well.

TRY THIS

Turn cleaning time into spa time. It seems that a major complaint of almost all women today is never having enough time to do nice things for themselves—to spoil themselves a little. So in the true spirit of multitasking, give yourself beauty treatments while cleaning house! Why not? Put healing lotion on your hands or conditioning oil on your cuticles before you put on your rubber gloves to wash the dishes. Put foot cream on under cotton socks. Put a deep conditioner on your hair and a masque on your face and get busy! Chances are you don't look your very best to clean your house anyway, and this way, once your home is beautiful and rejuvenated, a quick shower will leave you soft, smooth, beautiful, and rejuvenated as well!

zen concept

mantra for meditation in the cleaning of floors

We have walked a thousand
miles on the floor of this home.
Make the footprints we leave
here ones of kindness and love.

haiku for sweeping, mopping, and running the vacuum cleaner

family take flight
with your feet planted firmly
on this heart of mine.

cleaning koan
who is the face
in the mirror?

SIX.

THE ONES YOU LOVE

*I*t is often a search to understand ourselves better that leads to any effort at self-improvement, and probably what led you to this book—a desire to find a new approach to some of the age-old issues you have with keeping house. You ask yourself, "Why do I struggle with this?" or "Why is it so easy for Betty to keep house and so difficult for me?!" The answer lies in the mirror. You have to get a grip on who you are, what your strengths are, where your weaknesses lie, and most importantly, what it is that will motivate you to strive for improvement.

When I look in the mirror, I see a woman who has accomplished a great deal, has great dreams for the future, and whose deepest desire at *this moment in time* is to provide a happy, healthy home for my husband and children. My desires may be different tomorrow; they will almost certainly be different five years from now. But at this moment, the pursuit of that goal is what will bring me peace. That is what will bring me joy. Determining and embracing your purpose for keeping your home clean will help you understand yourself better and guide you toward the sixth factor of enlightenment that we are applying to housekeeping: *equanimity*. Focusing our attention on the ones that we love, and yes, *you* should be at the top of the list, helps us find that evenness of mind, especially under stress.

WHAT ROLE DO YOU PLAY?

I have been involved in theater in one form or another almost my entire life. I stole the show as the Cowardly Lion in a second-grade production of *The Wizard of Oz* and was hooked. One of the most wonderful aspects of acting is being able to shed your own identity, even for just a few minutes, and trying on the life of someone else. What does it feel like to be powerful, rich, old, alone, strong, or irreverent? We all have multiple facets to our personality and it's great fun, as well as oftentimes revealing, to explore those facets that we don't necessarily embrace in our daily lives. In real life, however, ultimately we want to come to the full awareness that the unique combination that is *us* is just fine. We are each one of a kind, spectacularly special individuals,

Buddha Says . . .

"You can search throughout the entire universe for someone who is more deserving of your love and affection than you are yourself, and that person is not to be found anywhere. You yourself, as much as anybody in the entire universe deserve your love and affection."

and at the same time we are one part of the whole of existence. We are one with everything.

Acting on the stage is fun. Putting on an act in real life is not. We all play many roles each day. Stop for a moment and consider what your list of roles looks like. Mine includes wife, mother, daughter, friend, chief cook and bottle washer, chauffeur, writer, and more. We move from role to role throughout the course of every day, often from moment to moment. It is a tough job! How much tougher do we make it on ourselves if we don't get to know what is at our own core? Often we spend so much time and energy trying to be what others want us to be or attempting to live up to some unrealistic expectation we have set for ourselves that we become frayed around the edges.

Zen Homemasters

"I truly believe that everybody over the age of two has to contribute and that it's not just one person's job; male-female, old-young, higher income-lower income. Everybody plays so everybody pays. It takes no special talent to clean a toilet and everybody uses it!"

—*Liz Craft*
School librarian, freelance writer, and mother of three
Monroe, Louisiana

These unrealistic expectations can be reflected in our feelings about our homes as well. We want our houses to look like a layout in a magazine, or we feel we can't rest until everything is spotless. Zen gives you permission to walk away from the expectations. You don't always have to be the funny one. No one but you expects you to always be in a good mood. Your house does not have to be perfect for others to find comfort there. It only has to be perfect for you. Ultimately it is up to each of us to become the woman we

want to be and portray the role that is
appropriate for us.

If by accident or by intention one
of your roles has become doing *every-*
thing for *everybody*, it's time to reconsider your casting decisions. It is one of
those conundrums found so frequently
in Zen that it is the very people that
cause the biggest messes that can be at
the foundation of your deepest desire
to *clean* the messes. Kids and cleaning?
Men that appreciate and assist with housework? How do we enlist
the assistance of the ones we love to tackle the jobs that we hate?

Keeping a house should not be about servitude. Keeping a
house clean and functioning smoothly should ideally be about service to one another—a cooperative effort to maintain the home
that sustains all that live within it. It should exist as a community
of caring people. Unfortunately we often fall short of this ideal.
Our goal in this chapter is to look for ways to refresh our system
and actively enlist the support and assistance of the people that
share our space.

TEACHING LIFE LESSONS

We are not doing the members of our family any favors by
doing everything for them. On multiple levels we are actually putting them at a disadvantage. First, you can only keep

up that level of service for so long before you grow angry and resentful. Unfortunately, that anger will taint your actions, thoughts, and feelings and you will take out your frustrations on those you want to embrace. Do not forget that anger is one of the five hindrances Buddha felt would block our pursuit of enlightenment.

You also don't allow other members of your family to realize their full potential if you do everything for them. How are your children ever going to learn to be independent and filled with self-esteem, learn the pride of ownership, and embrace the wonderful rewards of caring for their own possessions if you do everything for them? Sure you can do it faster and better, but you are taking away a huge opportunity to teach life lessons in personal growth. Raising a responsible child is far more important than speed cleaning. But how do you get them to do it?

As with most children, my children are creatures of habit. They like as many things as possible to be predictable—the same routines day in and day out. I think these patterns help them to feel safe in an uncertain world. Their minds and bodies are changing each day. There is so much to learn and see and do. They want to explore it all. They just need a base of safety and comfort to count on so that they can freely explore the world around them. If they are safe and secure, it allows their imagination and creativity to run wild and free. A relatively organized environment gives them this base. They don't know that they need it, and they will roll their eyes when you tell them it's room-cleaning time, but they will secretly enjoy a certain order.

I recently enrolled my daughter in her first dance class. I assumed that a roomful of three-year-old girls would be a circus. Not so! The rules of the dance studio were made very clear from the outset and they are reviewed regularly. There is a system in place for entering the studio, placing your bag in the proper location, reporting to your appointed spot on the floor, switching from tap shoes to ballet shoes, and so forth. When I recently observed class, it ran like a well-oiled machine. The framework was so firmly engrained that it freed those beautiful little dancers to explore their creativity and learn the art of dance. The experience reminded me of the absolute necessity to instill a system in my home, even for its youngest members. If the dance instructors can get twelve little girls to tap-dance, surely I can get my children to pick up their rooms!

Comedian Phyllis Diller once said, "Cleaning your house while your kids are still growing is like shoveling the walk before it stops snowing." While this may be true, it is not too much to ask that children keep their messes to a minimum and restricted to a specific area of the house—their rooms (and perhaps a playroom if you are lucky enough to have this luxury). Allow them to make their space their own within bounds of reason. You don't

Zen Homemakers

"I do love to be organized. I have to have a sense of balance and like for the house to run smoothly. Not to say that we don't have chaos every now and then, because we do. We all have meltdowns and when they occur, I just stop—look at the beautiful little faces around me—and thank God for such blessings."

—*Mamie Nelson*
Customer service manager,
community volunteer,
mother of two
West Monroe, Louisiana

have to tell them that you are teaching them to clean their rooms Zen style, but respect the fact that while their rooms are a part of your house, to them, it is their whole world. In Zen, everything possesses this duality. Everything is at once part of the big picture and yet it is a piece or parcel with its own individual integrity as well.

Zen Homemasters

"I try not to go to bed with my toddler's toys all over the house. I make sure we clean up before bedtime. No matter how much a pain it is at night, I'm always glad in the morning. Plus, he learns (hopefully) not to be a slob."

—*Jennifer Sutherland*
Office manager/marketing
coordinator, mother of one
Stillwater, Oklahoma

- Let them decorate their spaces and help develop an organizational system that is their own. Who says that everything has to be folded and in the chest of drawers? If your son likes his T-shirts stacked on a shelf in the closet, so be it.
- Make sure little hands can access the places their toys are to be stored.
- Put a bar in their closet within reach and buy hangers in your children's favorite colors.
- Allow them to have as much ownership of the space as possible.

Get down on their level and make cleaning up as easy as possible for them. Your children see the world in a totally different way than you do and from a completely different eye level. Get on your hands and knees and observe their world the way they do. Do they have drawers that are easy for them to open and close? Are their storage containers colorful and enticing? Do they know where their books go and are they able to reach the bookshelves that you have provided for them? Let them dust the bottom shelves. Put their snacks at the bottom of the refrigerator or pantry. Get kids miniature cleaning supplies that fit their little hands and bodies. They may not be able to fold adult-size towels so teach them to fold washcloths and hand towels.

"In the job of home-keeping there is no raise from the boss and seldom praise from others to show us we have hit the mark. Except for the child, woman's creation is so often invisible."
—*Anne Morrow Lindbergh,* Gift from the Sea

Young children learn visually. It is the sights that they see and not the words that they hear you say that make the greatest impression on them, so once you have their rooms at an agreed-upon level of neatness and organization, take pictures of the space. Then post those pictures in that area as a visual reference for them. If they can see what the space should look like and can remember that they helped you get it that way, they are much more likely to be able to repeat the task. Plus, you can turn it into a fun game—how long will it take you to get your room to look just like the pictures we took? And games are always effective in helping your child to clean their space. The majority of children love to be timed in their efforts. They like to count along with you

Seeds of Rapture

Give your children every opportunity to be self-sufficient but make sure that you are setting them up for success. They'll be happier and much more helpful.

the number of items they've placed into their toy chests. And they love hugs for a job well done.

When it comes to common living space, it is the clutter that can kill you, and the mess that kids can create is amazing in its scope. If you don't keep it under control, the kid clutter can get out of hand in a hurry. At our house the policy is that only one toy, the one each child is actively playing with, can be brought into the main living space. If one of the children wants to get something else, the first toy has to go back into its place.

Small children are still trainable. What about teenagers? Trying to get teenagers to do *anything* you want them to do is like trying to herd cats. The only thing that worked for me with my teenage stepson was to appeal to his growing desire for independence. One approach was that his chores had to be done before he could go out. That usually worked relatively well. Trying to

Zen Homemasters

"I am training my children (sixteen, thirteen, and eleven) in basic living skills, so of course that includes housework. It would be easier to just do it myself, but I do feel it's important to allow them to contribute to the duties of the household. It is important not to have them taken care of by someone else. I just feel it is part of my responsibility in raising responsible kids."

—*Laura Evans Muckleroy*
mother of three
West Monroe, Louisiana

teach him to engage in the "life skills" he would need when living out on his own was a bit more difficult. I met with resistance at every turn, until finally I realized that I *was* trying to train him to live out in the real world—so I just *told* him that's what I was doing. And for whatever reason, when I would engage in a housekeeping lesson by saying this was something he would need in the near future when he had his own place, he perked right up, paid attention, and got really good at housework.

JOURNEY TOGETHER

Last fall. Kindergarten. I finally heard the words I had been dreading since my son's birth. "We really need to work on his organizational skills." Oh no, I thought to myself at first. He has it too. He's messy! He's unorganized! This will plague him his entire life! Then I took a deep breath and looked down at my angelic five-year-old, realized it wasn't a lost cause just yet, smiled at the kindergarten teacher and said, "Okay. We'll work on it!"

My son is on a journey, too, and his is just beginning. Perhaps in order to produce a more compassionate (not to mention organized and knowledgeable about how to clean a house and do laundry) man for future generations of women, we have to start with our sons. All the sons of today are the husbands and fathers of tomorrow. With the tools we are learning and the awareness we are finding as we strive for enlightenment, we can help our sons *and* daughters overcome organizational challenges now so that in the future their path will be easier toward becoming the men and women we know they are capable of being. Maybe we should even teach them to meditate!

IT'S A MAN'S JOB

Men want to contribute. They just often don't know how. Men are also quick to remind us that they are not mind readers. We want them to be, but this is a skill they have just not mastered. Therefore, we have to ask.

One of women's greatest strengths, that works completely to our disadvantage, is to make the doing of everything look easy. We can cook supper with a baby on our hip, talk on the phone to our son's teacher, hear the buzzer sound indicating that the laundry in the dryer is done, unload the dryer and switch the wash over into it, and still manage a whispered "How was your day?" when our husband walks in. However, just as

Zen Homemasters

"He (my husband) works hard to keep us in a beautiful neighborhood and home and we shouldn't trash it! When the housecleaning is not an issue it also leaves more time for the important things—romance, movie time, outdoor activities. It is my job to make him feel like he is King of the world that I actually rule."

—*Bonalyn Boyd*
Mother of two, full-time creative services director for her church, freelance designer, community volunteer, and part-time opera singer Fleming Island, Florida

with our Zen practice, it takes effort to make things look effortless. Men think we've got it all under control and don't want to get in our way. We have to ask for the help we need, and our significant others may still not "get it." They will never understand how much we want and need their help and how wonderful it would be if their help were lent to us spontaneously. They will probably grumble and complain, but who cares? As long as it gets done. Sure it would be wonderful if your mate would just jump up and lend a hand without being asked. But men and women are just different that way. And what fun would life be if we were all the same? Define what needs to be done in your home, communicate clearly and without emotion if possible (men don't respond well to "irrational female emotions"), and ask for help. Ask and you shall receive (at least most of the time). My husband actually requested that I make a written list of things I need him to accomplish. If that's what it takes, I have no problem with it! If they don't get it, fine. Ask for their help anyway. Nine times out of ten you will get the support that you need.

"The same passions in man and woman nonetheless differ in tempo; hence man and woman do not cease misunderstanding one another."
—Friedrich Nietzsche, the German existential philosopher

In an article titled "The Future of Marriage," a writer with the International Future Trends states, "The biggest stress on marriage in the late twentieth century is a transition from a clear cut gender-based division of labor to a much less focused one. For a century or more, men were assigned to the work force and women to domestic duties. This social arrangement is becoming defunct."

In *Domestic Revolutions, A Social History of American Family Life*, Dr. Steven Mintz writes, "Men's and women's domestic roles are not ordained by human nature, biology, or men's and women's psychology. Rather, they are the product of particular historical circumstances, social processes, and ideologies, and vary widely by race, religion and time period."

Today's men seem just as confused as women about how to cope with the constantly changing expectations of life in the modern world. All the rules have changed over the course of the last 100 or so years and they are just as baffled by where they stand in the big scheme of things as we are. The time period in which we live is changing rapidly. Sometimes it's difficult to adjust, let alone if the expectations of your role have changed entirely. Just fifty years ago, most men understood their place in the world clearly. They went out into the world, they worked nine to five, they came home for dinner and to read the newspaper, watch a little TV, and go to bed. They had been accustomed to being the clear-cut leader of the family unit. Before that, in our preindustrial agrarian days, all members of the family lived and worked together. In a relatively short period of

Zen Homemasters

"Marriage is a job in itself. Both husband and wife need to have the same goals and work toward those goals. Both have to give 100 percent effort to everything; marriage, children, jobs, cooking, cleaning, etc. Communication is the key to life, love and the pursuit of domestic tranquility."

—*Marilyn Bryant*
Corporate retail trainer and mother of two teenage daughters Bossier City, Louisiana

time we booted men off the family farm and said, "Go out and earn a living. I'll do all the rest." Now we are all of a sudden saying, "Come back to the home—be sensitive and understand my needs. Help me clean the house and bathe the kids, and by the way, I make just as much money as you do and don't really need you around anyway, so you better get it together!" Men have it tough too.

THE ODD COUPLE

It was the inspiration for the original *Odd Couple*, the fodder for a multitude of today's sitcoms, the subject of many magazine articles, and a fact of life—quite often, opposites attract. It seems that we may be subconsciously searching for a mate who will balance us and perhaps make up for the qualities we feel we lack. And while this balancing act may work for you on a number of levels, when it comes to your approach to cleaning the house, being at complete attitudinal odds with your partner can create a great deal of stress. What do we do if we have been attracted to our opposite? Something's got to give. In a relationship of domestic opposites, communication and clearly expressing your needs is going to be even more crucial to the success of the household and ultimately to the partnership itself.

Look at living with your opposite as an opportunity to learn from them rather than as a personal mission to change them. Develop compromises and cooperate with one another, making maximum use of each partner's best qualities. And educate your partner on the need to live the Middle Way, keeping in mind that neither extreme—fanatical cleanliness nor slovenly sloppiness—will lead you to enlightenment.

The flip side of this coin, that "birds of a feather flock together," can be equally difficult when it comes to divvying up domestic duties. Two clean freaks can drive each other to distraction and two slobs can create a home that is virtually unlivable. In this situation, awareness and self-knowledge will be the keys to tranquility. Determine together the level of order (or disorder) that is acceptable to you both, and create a plan to get you there.

MOTIVATING MEN

One awakening that is motivating men today is that many of them are realizing that they are missing out on an integral part of their lives by being relatively uninvolved in the raising of their children. It's no longer enough for them that their only responsibility to their family be pursuit of the almighty dollar. Conversely, women are being reminded that they are just as capable of pursuing the almighty dollar as a man. Both men and women can drive carpools and change diapers. Both men and women can serve as

Zen Homemasters

"I am a slob married to a neat freak, which you would think would be a good thing, but it is probably the one thing we butt heads about. I just believe that a messy house is the sign of a happy family. At the end of my life I want to look back and know that my kids, my husband, my friends, and I were all happy and had fun. Not that I had a clean house."

—*Melissa McGrath*
Freelance editor, library
assistant, mother of three
Fountainville, Pennsylvania

CEOs of *Fortune* 500 companies or launch a successful start-up. And more and more often, if a couple is determining that it is in the best interest of their family for one or the other parent to stay at home, it is the father that is becoming the primary caregiver and homemaker.

There is a male equivalent to the assumption that women who stay home sit around eating bonbons and watching *Oprah* all day. Apparently men that have male friends staying at home with children assume that they get to sit around the house all day watching ESPN's *Sports Center* and drinking beer. Men also bring their unwillingness to ask for directions to the art of at-home parenting.

The stay-at-home dad is not yet an everyday occurrence, but men and women having a more equitable division of labor on the home front is becoming the norm rather than the exception. While most of us are not raising our own food and milking our own cows, we are working together for the good of the cause (our families), and erasing the lines that divide domestic responsibilities by gender. That is a future trend that is definitely worth continuing.

Dads don't have to be at home full-time in order for their children to reap dramatic benefits from their presence and involvement around the house. Sociologists at the University

Zen Homemasters

"Any working woman should have a housekeeper. This frees up time for sex. Who has time for love-making when there are commodes waiting to be disinfected?"

—*Patti Nelson*
Community relations manager
and mother of one
West Monroe, Louisiana

of California's Riverside campus have shown that "school aged children who do housework with their fathers are more likely to get along with their peers and have more friends. What's more, they are less likely than other kids to disobey teachers or make trouble at school and are less depressed or withdrawn." Yardwork, washing dishes, any activity that contributes to the betterment of the household strengthens the bonds within the family and particularly with the male parent, providing children with security and an image of cooperation in action for them to emulate.

If the man in your life needs more motivation to get in the game and clean, show him this paragraph. A man cleaning is sexy! What if we could convince men that they are at their absolute sexiest when they help us clean or burp the baby? What will it take for them to understand that if they put a load of clothes into the washing machine now it will pay off in the bedroom later? It is by no means the act of cleaning that is a turn-on for a woman; it is the outward expression of love, the visible action that shows a man is not just in it for the fun and good times. He can be a part of the not-so-glamorous, boring stuff too. A man cleaning speaks volumes about the way he feels about his partner.

What have we learned here about getting the men in our lives to help with the cleaning? They are never going to get it, so just forget it. Communicate clearly and ask for the help you need. Explain that their children will get beaten up at school a lot less often if they clean the house. And if all else fails, bribe them with sex.

MAKING SELF-CARE A PRIORITY

The theme of this chapter is focusing on the ones you love and internalizing the factor of enlightenment equanimity. But how can you be expected to develop equanimity, a sense of balance and calm in the face of great stressors, if your self-care is such a low priority that it didn't even make the list?

Life is like an oxygen mask on an airplane. The flight attendant instructs you that in case of a loss in cabin pressure, the masks will drop from the ceiling. You are instructed to place your mask on first and then assist any child traveling with you. Well, the attendant has just given each of us a set of metaphorical instructions on living a happy life. If we do not take care of ourselves first, we will be unable to care for others.

As natural-born caregivers with this tendency reinforced by our culture and societal expectations, we tend to put the needs of everyone else before our own. We put a smile on our face and insist to everyone that asks that "everything is fine." The truth? We are trying to accomplish alone what would, in most other cultures, take many to accomplish. We are working, raising children, supporting spouses, running households, and furthering careers. We, and those around us, expect us to accomplish it all without complaint. Is it any wonder we are exhausted, unhappy, and on pharmaceuticals (or a combination of all three) just to get through the day?

We must move ourselves back up the priority list. Asking for assistance doesn't make you a failure. It makes you smart and assertive. Pampering yourself does not make you spoiled. It feeds your spirit. Going to bed a little early or taking time after dinner to take a long walk makes you better able to care for those who rely on your strength. If we can utilize our time caring for our homes to nourish our souls and spirits, it will help return us to sanity, and self-care can automatically become a part of every day of our lives.

TRY THIS

Contain yourself. Make sure you have plenty of baskets, boxes, and containers to control the stuff that you have deemed worthy of keeping in your home. Children, men, and those of us that are domestically challenged need lots of guidance and perform better if things are kept simple and straightforward. One way to simplify organization is to ensure that things are either clearly labeled or that their purpose is extremely obvious. Make it easy for shoes to go in the right place. Color-code baskets for everybody. Use your creativity and the plethora of products in the market today to make a place for everything. And make as many organizational tools as possible portable. "Junk" tends to travel. What was in the bedroom yesterday finds itself in the living room today and on the bathroom or kitchen counter tomorrow. Portability of containers adds to the ease of transport and likelihood that the stuff that has traveled will eventually find its way back home.

TRY THIS II

Regardless of age, playing games is fun. Perhaps if you take some of the "work" out of housework and make it more of a game you play with yourself it will change the nature of the way you feel about the tasks you do around your home. Set a timer for fifteen minutes and see what you can get done. Give everybody in the family a list of three chores to accomplish. Whoever gets done first and rings a bell or hits a buzzer in a central location gets to choose where you go to dinner that night.

mantra for meditation on men and children

Do not let me forget that i am cleaning this home for them and that i too am worthy of a clean home.

haiku dedicated to the ones we love

i look into your eyes
i see all that is to be
in today and now

SEVEN.

THE THINGS YOU LOVE

*F*or far too many of us, it is clutter that fills our empty spaces. We are trying to fill some void, either psychological or emotional, with accumulated belongings, be it books or clothes or decorative knickknacks or piles of unfolded laundry. Some of us try to fill our empty spaces with food, alcohol, or other unhealthy addictions. These may not take up space on your shelves, but it is clutter nonetheless.

The truth of the matter is that there is no possession that will ever fill that empty space. We need to learn to see and understand the value of emptiness. If we can weed through some of the tangible barricades of possessions that we feel are protecting us—from loss, from loneliness, from something we cannot identify—we can begin to refill our empty spaces with what they really should be full of: love, laughter, creative pursuits, adventure, or perhaps just a little peace. This chapter will provide you with guidance on getting rid of the items that clutter up your home and life and how to care, mindfully, for what is left.

Cutting through the clutter to the point where everything around you is beautiful, meaningful, or functional will instill in you the true essence of the last factor of enlightenment that we will explore: *rapture*. Rapture is probably the factor that is hardest to define and most intimidating to someone new to the Zen approach to life. Some define rapture as a religious experience, one in which they know and understand some divine truth. That's a lot to ask from keeping house! For our purposes, let's think of rapture as being carried away or overwhelmed by emotion, usually joy.

In a well-loved home, the opportunity for this type of rapture exists daily. It is in dusting the frame of a picture of your last family vacation or the paperweight that your best friend brought you when she visited England. It is in cleaning the mirror that each family member glances at as they make sure they are presentable to go out into the world each day. It is in polishing the end tables that are home to the magazines you will read or the glass of iced tea you will sip as you talk to a faraway friend or relative. Feelings of rapture are yours for the taking when you are actively surrounding yourself with things that are truly and deeply meaningful or beautiful to you and in the processes of caring for them each day, allowing yourself to be reminded of the meaning or the moment that they signify.

IS THE GLASS HALF FULL OR HALF EMPTY?

Lao Tse was not a Buddhist. He is considered the leading figure of another Far Eastern school of philosophy known as Taoism. The *Tao Te Ching* is the pre-eminent text expressing Taoist beliefs and focuses in large part on the value of emptiness. It points out that a wheel is made up of many spokes, but if it weren't for the empty space in the middle, the wheel could not and would not serve its purpose. You can see a water pitcher and assume that its value is in being a pitcher. But what truly gives it its value is the empty space inside. If it were unable to carry water, its purpose would be something very different, or perhaps it would serve no purpose at all.

In college, I was an interior design major . . . for one semester. My thought was that I would combine my love of psychology with my creativity and design fabulously functional workspaces that would encourage others in their pursuit of professional success and personal fulfillment. After that one semester I realized I was not cut out to be an interior designer. Interior design majors had to not only take art history and textile courses, but they also had to take a battery of architecture and mechanical engineering courses as well. Nope! Not for me! I transferred to the College of Communications and received my degree in organizational communication. As I pursued my career in marketing, things I had learned during that one semester of interior design course work stayed with me, particularly in the graphic design of advertising campaigns and layout of marketing and sales materials. Elements of good design transcend the fields in which they are utilized. What makes an ad eye-catching and effective are the same things that make the design of interiors work, and the most important element to consider is the use of positive and negative space. The two must work in harmony and each is necessary to accentuate the whole. What is not there is just as important as what is.

Japanese arts and culture are full of examples of utilizing positive and negative space. Calligraphy, ink paintings, and rock gardens are all about the formation of images around what is *not* there. The background is not an afterthought—it is an integral part of the picture, the lettering, or the placement of stones in a symbolic manner. This Zen aesthetic, the artistic elements that are considered beautiful by those that practice the philosophy, is expressed in the Japanese word *kanso*, loosely translated as "simplicity." But kanso is far more complicated than that. It is the belief that true beauty is achieved by the elimination or omission of things. As we look around our homes and seek a state of rapture, how can we eliminate that which is unnecessary? How can we omit items that do not lead us toward our ultimate goal of enlightenment?

"Take care of things, and they will take care of you."
—*Shunryu Suzuki, Zen Master*

When our shelves are covered with knickknacks, our drawers are stuffed to overflowing, and our countertops covered in rarely used accumulations, we are only able to focus on what is there.

There is no space for newer and potentially better possessions to enter.

Zen is certainly not about the accumulation of "stuff"; however, truly valuing the stuff you've got is *very* Zen in nature. Think again about the concept of positive and negative space. What items in your home do you treasure so much that they should have a place of honor, free from other clutter that might detract from their importance? When you ask the question, "Is this item truly of value to me?" what is your answer? Does it make my life better in some way? Is it meaningful to me? It will be easier to toss the things that don't measure up to this standard. "I hate this pillow but it goes with the couch" is *not* reason enough to keep it and allow it to take up valuable space in your home and in your life. Toss it!

THE COST OF CLUTTER

For those who have clutter issues, the accumulated stuff serves, in their mind, as a safety net. Somehow you feel that it protects you from reality. The reality is that the clutter you have accumulated

Living One with Nature

Combine a cup of olive oil with half a cup of lemon juice and use with a lint-free cloth to polish hardwood furniture.

is costing you dearly—in one of the places it can hurt the most: your pocketbook.

Do you find yourself wasting time at home or at work doing things twice because you didn't do them correctly the first time or were unable to find a key piece of information that was necessary to complete the task? Are there parts of your home, for which you are paying a pretty penny, that are unusable for their intended purpose because they are full of stuff? A lot of clutter bugs buy items that they already had in their home but just couldn't locate. They may overbuy food and perishable products and then wind up throwing away food that has spoiled because they couldn't use it all in time. An overabundance of clutter can lead to a lack of organization that causes you to miss the deadline for paying bills. You are then forced to pay late fees or a check can bounce because you weren't able to determine your correct balance. The high-ticket items that you own such as your home and vehicles can depreciate in value if they are not properly maintained. Lost library books alone can cost you a fortune!

These are the tangible costs of clutter, but what of the spiritual cost? Are you familiar with that feeling of being frazzled and distracted, frustrated that you can't find what you are looking for, always harried and rushed to arrive at places on time when you spend precious moments looking for your other black shoe or socks that match? Do you snap at your children because they can't locate homework? Do you and your spouse have recurring arguments about items that can't be located? These feelings are amping up your adrenaline, tightening your muscles, raising your blood pressure,

Seeds of Rapture

The decluttering process you are undertaking can and should be one of the most reverential and meditative that you have experienced on your Zen Housekeeping journey thus far. For every old toy, outdated piece of clothing, and expired lip liner that you have tossed out, you are one step closer to enlightenment. Consider the physical act of decluttering as parallel to the spiritual decluttering that is taking place as you live in the moment, eliminate hindrances, and develop a newfound appreciation for all that you are and all that you have.

and sapping your energy. Just as negative thoughts are as real and powerful to your brain as actual negative experiences, stress over a mess is just as impactful on your mind and body as stress over a deadline at work, finances, or over a relative who is ill.

USING ZEN TO GET IN THE ZONE

Professional organizers recommend that in both the process of clearing clutter as well as regular cleaning, you divide living spaces into zones. This is particularly effective in large spaces that may serve multiple purposes, like your living room. There may be a reading zone, a zone for listening to music, or a television-viewing zone for example. All your remote controls should be centrally located in the zone for television viewing. Books and magazines shouldn't migrate to all four corners of the room and clutter every surface. They should be placed neatly, with a plan in mind and the right tools for the job such as shelves or magazine baskets, in the reading zone. Headphones, CD cases, stereo, and remotes should all be placed in the music zone. This provides a direction for you when you are trying to determine what goes where. If you come across an item that doesn't seem to have a place, consider your zones again. Does this item need to be there or can you get rid of it altogether? Do you need to designate another zone?

To maximize the effectiveness of this zone system, make sure you have the right furniture, lighting, and accessories to make each zone truly able to fulfill its purpose.

This "zone" system is similar to the educational strategy used by educators for small children. Most preschool and elementary school rooms are set up in centers. You can play and work in the art center, the kitchen center, the reading center, etc. Children respond to the center system because it is clear and it makes sense. There are specific places where specific activities take place. The result will be the same if you effectively designate zones in your home. It will make sense, increase efficiency, and allow everyone to know where items can be found and where the items should be returned after they are used.

So how does designating these zones in your house relate to getting in "The Zone"? You primarily hear this term in reference to top-performing athletes. When a basketball player seems to be making every shot almost effortlessly, when a kicker makes every single field goal including the game winner with three seconds left on the clock, when an ice skater executes every jump and maintains flawless artistry as well, they are said to be in "the zone." The Zone occurs when you are completely focused on a task. Time

Seeds of Rapture

The only prescription bottles that should be in your home are those containing medication you or a member of your family are currently taking.

seems to stand still. You feel you are at the perfect place at that moment in time. You lose all fear, doubt, and misgivings. You are at one with all that is around you and feel completely at peace. Getting in the Zone for even a few fleeting moments gives us a taste of the quality we are striving for in the practice of Zen Housekeeping. These moments are glimpses of enlightenment in our otherwise unpredictable world.

You may find yourself in the Zone when engaged in a hobby or doing work that you are really passionate about. As you meditate, that feeling of freedom is what you are striving to achieve. Housekeeping is probably still not your favorite endeavor, but the opportunity is there to embrace the experience and transcend the ordinary to find a place of meaning in the mundane. Moments in the Zone cannot be forced. However, you can lay the groundwork for their occurrence. That is what all our efforts to systemize and strategize our housekeeping efforts are leading to—creating the opportunity for more moments of true joy and great peace. How much better can life be for you and your loved ones if you create a home that allows all to operate at their maximum potential?

Clearing away the clutter is a critical step on the path toward living enlightened. You must commit to the process and get ruthless in your efforts to rid yourself of accumulations. How do you do it? Get trashy!

- You know in your heart that about half the stuff you own can be thrown out. Peruse your house with a trash bag. If it's broken, ugly, or irritating, pitch it immediately. If it hasn't been worn, used, or eaten in the course of a year, out it goes. If you've been saying you would sew the button back on for more than six months, toss it!

- Throw away anything in your home that has passed its expiration date. This can be refrigerated or canned food, cleaning supplies, or over-the-counter medications. If you can't find an expiration date, throw it away. Chances are it is no longer effective.

- Pull out your makeup drawer. Now dump it all in a trash bag and start fresh. Makeup does not stay fresh forever. You can spread bacteria to your eyes from antiquated mascara or old eyeliners, and the oils in many types of makeup can separate and change consistency as well as color. Dump it all and go get a makeover. Purchase new, fresh products and applicators. You will feel like a new woman.

- Open up your jewelry box and pull out anything that is tacky or tangled. Can that necklace be untangled? Is it worth it to try? If the answer is no, it's outta there. One caveat on throwing away jewelry: If it is made of a precious metal or contains a genuine stone, don't throw it out. Take it to a jeweler and see if they can get the knot out or advise you on a way to use the piece as the basis for something new or melt it down for you. Also, little girls love playing dress-up. You might want to save a few pieces of costume jewelry or fun clothes if you have little girls in your life. But limit it to just a few items!

TO DECLUTTER,
BEGIN WITH THE END IN MIND

I've touched here on a few of the basics of beginning your decluttering process. Now let's get down to specifics—the nuts and bolts of decluttering your home, one room at a time. For decluttering efforts to be truly effective, it is helpful to have a vision of what you ultimately want to accomplish. What do you want the given space to look like when you are finished? What purpose do you want the space to serve? Work toward a room that only includes true treasures or functional and frequently used tools. Make sure the room is set up for maximum productivity and well equipped to serve the function for which it was designed.

Buddha Says . . .
"There are only two mistakes one can make along the road to truth; not going all the way, and not starting."

CLUTTER IN THE KITCHEN

Due to its role as the heart of the home, the kitchen frequently serves as a clutter collecting space. Often our kitchens are either logistically located in the center of our homes, or they are the first place that we stop whenever we enter. Keys get dropped on the counter. Incoming and outgoing mail gets dropped there. Papers, projects, and planners along with clipped coupons, calendars, and "to do" lists, grocery lists, and more clutter our countertops. That's all before we ever even begin cooking. What about coffeepots, toasters, can openers, spices, and fruit bowls that add to the confusion in our kitchen? Where do we begin?

Set aside some time, probably a couple of hours, where you can work without major interruption. When you are ready to undertake a major project such as this, send the rest of the family off to a movie or sporting event. They will have fun and it ensures you have the time you need to see the project through to completion. After their departure, clear off your kitchen table and then pull out all your drawers and dump them on the table. Pull up a trash can and get to work.

- First, throw away all the packets of restaurant ketchup and soy sauce. You are never going to use them!
- The same goes for the hermetically sealed packets of plastic silverware with the salt and pepper inside. They might come in handy for that picnic you are planning to take one day, but your peace of mind is more important than being well prepared for a picnic that may or may not ever occur. Pitch them!
- Any storage containers that do not have a matching lid go in the garbage next (unless they can be recycled).
- Weed through all the tools and utensils and toss out any that are broken in any way or that you don't use on a regular basis.
- Kitchen towels with holes or stains need to either be trashed or added to your cleaning caddies to be used for polishing or dusting.

- Wipe out all your empty drawers with a damp sponge and if they need it, reline them with new shelf paper. That rubbery stuff that prevents items from slipping is excellent and it doesn't require you to figure out how to use any type of adhesive. Just cut it to the proper size and place it inside.

Now you are ready to begin adding back the drastically pared-down contents of your drawers, continuing to toss items that you come across that you may have missed in the first round of disposing or that you have now decided have no place in your new and improved kitchen.

With your drawer clutter decreased, you are ready to tackle your cabinets. The first step here is to dispose of dishes that are chipped, cracked, or broken. It is amazing how many chipped plates make their way back into your cabinets. They are not just unattractive, however. They can be dangerous and unhealthy. Once a bowl or plate has a chip, the chipped area will be much more vulnerable to further damage and miniscule chips can find

Living One with Nature

The long-term effects of particles from plastics seeping into food has still not been fully determined. So why not err on the side of caution? If your plastic products have been compromised in any way, dispose of them. Some research indicates that the plastic wrap that seals food we buy from our local grocery store may be one of the most potentially harmful plastic products to which we are regularly exposed. If you want to be vigilant about your health, remove these products from their store-bought packaging and rewrap them in cellophane wrap instead.

their way into your food. Additionally, the material that was origi-
nally used for the piece before it was glazed is usually unknown
and it could possibly allow toxins to leach into your food. Ditch
those dishes! Any cracked glasses should also be disposed of for
the same reasons.

In your pantry, what foods are you never going to use? Perhaps
you purchased some items when you were on that Indian cooking kick, or your kids used to love SpaghettiO's but now won't
touch them. Whatever the reason, place any nonperishables that
you are not going to use in a box and take them to a local food
bank or women's shelter. Get rid of half-empty packages that have
wound up in the very back of your food storage space. If there is
one serving left in the bottom of a bottle, toss it. Go through the
same process in your refrigerator, paying particular attention to
expiration dates. Wash refrigerator drawers, doors, and shelving
with a mild, nontoxic, and food-friendly soap. It's a good practice
to line the bottoms of vegetable and fruit bins with paper towels
and replace them regularly.

Take a look at your pots, pans, and bake ware. If the bottoms of
pans are damaged they can affect the taste of food cooked in them
or possibly expose you to hazardous contaminants. If handles are
broken or a matching lid cannot be found, get rid of them too.

The last things to think about before you can consider your
kitchen decluttering complete are the appliances and accoutre-
ments that reside on the countertops. Maybe when you feel you
have embraced this new less-cluttered lifestyle you can begin to
leave a few items out for easy access, but for now adhere to the "a

Seeds of Rapture

If you are a hard-core clutterer, it is in your best interest to find a place to store *everything* underneath your counters and have a completely clear countertop. If you leave one thing out, it will attract other things like a magnet and before you know it, you will have lost control again.

place for everything and everything in its place" philosophy and get it all out of view. If you are further along your home organization path, you can leave a few items, either decorative or utilitarian, on the countertops.

One advantage of clearing out your kitchen is that it's a great excuse to shop for replacements that you like better or are more in tune with your new way of life. Do not buy products just to buy them or you will find yourself drowning in clutter all over again, but we all deserve attractive and functional tools to populate the heart of our home. Beautiful and affordable options abound.

BATHROOM DECLUTTERING BASICS

Just as in the kitchen, it will be your drawers and cabinets that require the most attention in your bathrooms, and I recommend a similar system for eliminating clutter. Dump everything out and go item by item, evaluating its usefulness and necessity, ensuring that expiration dates are being honored and that the lotions and potions that cover your counter or congest the cabinets underneath your sinks are things you actually use. Each bathroom should have its own individual first-aid kit, or at least a well-stocked medicine cabinet containing fresh supplies of Band-Aids, antibiotic creams, hydrogen peroxide, rubbing alcohol, and other basics. It's a good idea to also have a pain reliever, fever reducer, and something for nausea that is age appropriate for each member of the family.

The frequent use of towels and washcloths and their constant laundering guarantees that they will get worn out relatively quickly, and nothing makes a bathroom look more neglected than ratty, ragged towels. Review your supply regularly (I try to pay close attention when I'm folding and get them out of circulation then—old towels can be included in your outdoor cleaning caddy for use when you are washing your car or doing other outside cleaning projects) and renew them as needed with fresh and fluffy replacements.

CLOSET CLUTTER

Closets are one of the toughest areas to clear of clutter for a number of reasons. First is the sheer magnitude of clothes and shoes and belts and purses and scarves and jackets and sweaters and swimsuits that we have accumulated over the course of our adult lives. Closets contain many items that have great sentimental value and also items that have a lot of emotional and psychological meaning for us. We keep our fat clothes in case we gain back the ten pounds we worked so hard to lose. We keep our skinny clothes just in case we actually do get back down to that size again. Your husband can't bear to part with his letterman's jacket. Your childbearing days are behind you, but you looked so cute in that maternity muumuu that you wore when you were expecting. Are

Seeds of Rapture

Keep an eye on store circulars and white sale ads. Towels are almost always on sale somewhere, so there is no need to buy low-quality towels or to break the bank buying the "good stuff."

you still harboring hopes that your daughter will one day wear your wedding gown? She will be her own unique woman with her own unique style. She should be free from the expectation that she will walk down the aisle in *your* wedding dress.

Our closets are landmines of memories. Again, you just have to remind yourself that your memories are not carried in the clothes; they are ever available to you in your heart. With that in mind, clear out all the things that have not been worn in a year or more, no longer fit, or have gone out of style. If you are holding on to certain dated pieces hoping that they will come back in style in some retro reincarnation or another, don't. Let it go! Donating them to a charitable organization is one option, but currently there is a proliferation of upscale consignment shops for every type of household item. Whether it's sports equipment, furniture, baby products and clothes, or clothes and accessories straight from your closet, chances are there is a store nearby that will resell them for you. Not only will you clear your closets, but you might also make a little spending money in the process. Check with consignment stores that interest you to find out their guidelines for items they will accept. Most are very choosy, so you can be sure of the quality of any item you might purchase there and also take heart that your pieces will find a good home.

ART SMARTS

When you have children, one of your greatest sources of joy, and one of the greatest sources of clutter, is their art. My children's artwork had become a real source of stress for me. It was piling up everywhere. I wanted it out and visible, but the refrigerator quickly became full. I thought about filing it for safe-keeping (and a sense of order), but that didn't honor the work they had done or the creativity they were showing.

Instead, we designed and premiered the Brownell Art Museum. They have a hallway that serves as the connecting corridor to each of their rooms and their bathroom. We bought a roll of thin cork-board and grosgrain ribbon and covered an entire wall in their hallway in the cork and framed it with the ribbon. Pushpins finished it off, and now we can hang their artwork as soon as it comes home from school or is completed at home. Once the wall is full, we consider the art exhibit complete and take a few pieces down (really special ones are filed at that point) to make room for new ones. The museum serves several purposes. It honors and displays their artwork, and it prevents me from drowning in piles of paper that I don't know what to do with but desperately want to keep. It's a great conversation piece when friends or family come over and makes use of a "wasted" space, a hallway that serves no other real purpose. Plus, the hall

Buddha Says . . .
"It is better to conquer yourself than to win a thousand battles. Then the victory is yours. It cannot be taken from you, not by angels or by demons, heaven or hell."

is now colorful and truly beautiful as it displays the work of my precious babies. Sometimes I'll paint or draw a picture too to add to the exhibit. You can put photos, reminders, calendars, stickers, chore charts, growth charts, and great report cards—anything you want—on your wall.

The art was one challenge that we managed to get under control. Arts and craft supplies were the other. Our kitchen table serves as our art center, so we dedicated a nearby pantry cupboard that wasn't being fully utilized to the safe-keeping of our supplies. Investing in several lidded plastic containers of various sizes also gave us a place to stow away everything from paints to crayons, Play-Doh, glue, glitter—everything we could possibly need for a project—and they stack neatly in the cupboard.

KIDS' ROOMS AND CLUTTER

Speaking of children, how do you ever get the clutter in their rooms under control?

First, get the children out of the house before you engage in this project. They will cry over every toy and piece of clothing and insist it is their absolute favorite. If you declutter while they are away, they will never miss the things you have discarded.

- Start by tossing the toys from Happy Meals and go from there. They are junk!
- If a toy is broken, torn, or irreparably stained, get rid of it.

- If critical pieces of the car-racing track or jigsaw puzzle are missing, trash the whole thing.
- Get rid of clothes that don't fit size-wise and get rid of the clothes that don't fit the people that your children are becoming.

Once you have a head start on clearing out the rooms of your children, utilize what remains to teach a loving lesson about the power of giving. Explain to your children that there are children in your town, your state, your country, our world, that don't have all the things that they do. Ask them to pick out a toy or two that they would like to give to a little boy or girl that may not have nice toys. Involve them in the process of taking your items, including those toys, to the charity of your choice for donation. Discuss with them the concept of giving—how good it feels to do nice things for others and how as you give things to others in a true spirit of sharing, it opens up space in your heart and your home for more good things to enter.

LETTING GO FOR THE GREATER GOOD

Pack rats are masters of deceit. Of course, the only person they are deceiving is themselves. We can convince ourselves that we will wear that orange plaid wraparound skirt in a size 2 one day. That book there, the one on the top shelf covered with dust, holds the answer to all life's questions. All those newspaper clippings? They are research for a project I am going to complete one day when I have time. Stop kidding yourself! One of the most powerful questions you can pose to yourself as you declutter and one that, if you are honest, will help you cut through a lot of the crap and get down to basics is, "Would this item be of greater value to someone else than it is to me?"

There is war, poverty, and starvation all over the world, and yet we need look no further than our own backyards to find people in need. Whenever you find something that doesn't fit, a book you'll never read, or a toy that bores your kids, put it in a place you have designated for Goodwill or the Salvation Army or another charity of your choice. Once it is in the Goodwill bag, *do not* reconsider your decision and get it back out again. You must also get the box or bag out of your house and to the charity drop-off. If you put the stuff in bags but it never makes it out of your house, it is still clutter, just in a different form. Make it a first of the month ritual to do a Goodwill dropoff. When you first

Buddha Says . . .

"Without violence, conscientious, full of compassion, let one only be desirous for the good of living beings."

begin the process of decluttering you may need to go once a week. The "recycling" of your old stuff is a karmic win-win. You are freeing up your space and you are assisting someone in need. Be sure to get a receipt for donated items, as your contributions are tax deductible.

Do you have high-tech items that you no longer use? Donate old computers to schools or homeless shelters. These organizations can get repairs done at low or no cost, and then the computers can be utilized by people who are truly in need. How great would it be for your old desktop computer, the one that you've replaced with a wi-fi laptop, to help provide technology training to an at-risk teen? What about old cell phones? By donating these to a shelter for battered women, you can provide a lifeline to the help and services needed for these women to start a new life. One word of caution, however: Clear your computer's hard drive and make sure that any personal information and all phone numbers have been deleted and that your cell phone service has been disconnected before you donate these items. This is simply for your protection in this unfortunate climate of fraud and identity theft. But don't let those concerns stop you from doing what you know is right.

CHARITABLE GIVING AND GAINING ENLIGHTENMENT

If you are still not convinced that giving unneeded or unused items to charity is the way to go, remind yourself that you are not just on a quest for a cleaner home. You are on a path of spiritual awakening as well. The essence of Zen is to achieve a state of enlightenment but it is also to make a positive impact on the world, or at least your part of it. In order to leave a place better than you found it, actions of charitable giving are a necessity and you should seek every possible opportunity to do good deeds.

Buddhism defines three ways in which one can give charitably. They are the giving of material wealth to good causes, providing sanctuary for people or animals that are in need, and spreading the knowledge of Buddha. This commitment to giving has been shown throughout time and across cultures and religions to be the most spiritually beneficial practice in which people can participate. It is only through the act of giving that you can receive, and through charitable acts you can transcend your own suffering and find peace and personal growth.

THE DUST BOWL

Once you have pared down your possessions to the clothes that fit, the books you really read (or treasure for some reason known only to you), the toys your kids actually play with, and the possessions that are truly meaningful, you need to keep them clean, and cleaning possessions requires dusting—with rapture in mind.

The best dust rag ever invented is the athletic sock. If you have socks with holes (and who doesn't?) or socks that are missing a mate, recycle them by adding them to your collection of cleaning supplies. Slip a sock over one hand and carry your bottle of

Seeds of Rapture

After your extensive decluttering efforts, the items left that require dusting should all be very meaningful to you. As you go about the process of dusting, pick up each item individually and caress it with your dust rag. Think about its meaning to you or its place of origin. Relive meaningful moments by practicing meaningful cleaning.

dusting solution in the other, and go forth and dust. With the sock on your hand, you can squeeze into small spaces and run your hand along the surfaces that you sometimes miss using a traditional duster. You can pick up individual treasures and caress their surfaces, reflecting on their meaning as you free them from the dust that has collected on them.

- Another handy dusting tool is the dryer sheets that you most likely already have in your cupboard. The quality of the sheets that help them eliminate static electricity in your laundry also serves as a magnet for dust particles.
- Cleaning glass or mirrors? Use a good-quality glass cleaner and either newspaper or coffee filters. This will help eliminate streaking and leave glass clear and shiny.
- Use a good-quality furniture polish for dusting your hardwood furniture but use it sparingly. Too much polish can leave a residue that will make wood appear cloudy and feel tacky to the touch.
- Never use regular soap or water on wood. It will dry, damage, and spot your quality furniture.
- Use the proper products for all those possessions that you cherish. It will lengthen their life and maximize the potential of their beauty.

Don't forget to dust difficult-to-reach or easily forgotten areas of your home. Tops of ceiling fan blades need regular attention as do the back of your television and home entertainment system. The tops of furniture may be out of sight, but the dust there can still cause sneezing and coughing and a lingering musty smell if you don't address it in a timely fashion. Using your vacuum cleaner's attachments, seasonally suck dust off the coils of your refrigerator and out of the lint trap on your clothes dryer. Want to minimize the amount of dust that accumulates in the first place? Open your windows as infrequently as possible and change your air filters monthly at a minimum. This will help save money on your heating and cooling bills as well.

A few other dusting tips:

- Always dust from top to bottom.
- Dust dry to wet. Dust the dry stuff off first before you use any liquid cleaners or furniture polish.
- The items that are at or around eye level will need to be dusted the most often. Dusting of really high and really low surfaces can be done less frequently but they still need to be dusted on a regular basis.
- Thoroughly dust all surfaces of electronic equipment regularly. This means picking up the DVD player and the computer keyboard for example and dusting not only underneath them, but also the bottoms of the items. Dust buildup can interfere with the internal workings of electronics, decrease their productivity and performance, and shorten the life of the product.

OPENING YOUR HOME TO WIND AND WATER

To this point, we've only looked at the necessity of ridding ourselves of possessions. But how do we work with the items that remain in order to create the best possible environment in our homes? One way to determine what you keep and how you place those items that remain in your home is through the utilization of feng shui.

Feng shui, literally translated as "wind and water," is a highly touted form of arranging your living and working space and is intended to foster the maximum in-and-out travel of chi, or the life force. A feng shui practitioner can assist you in the placement of objects (positive space) so that the chi can flow freely through the area that remains (negative space), or you can study the concepts of feng shui and do it yourself. Practitioners of this ancient art form also believe that all people are combinations of the elements found in nature—metal, earth, fire, water, and air. These experts say you will be happier and more successful if your home and office space allows the energy of nature to flow through it and that you will be more comfortable in your surroundings when you pay homage to and incorporate natural elements into your decorating. You should also make every effort to honor your own innate element-based style. Feng shui practitioners insist that the arrangement of your furniture and the addition of plants and mirrors to your decorating scheme can literally change your life.

Seeds of Rapture

Mirrors are one of the most popular items used in the implementation of feng shui. They are placed strategically throughout a space in order to reflect more of what the person wishes to attract.

If a misplaced piece of furniture can block the energy flow, just imagine what piles of clutter can do. But that is behind us now and you are free to move forward in your journey. You have removed the clutter and maximized the space available that is open and free from interference. Now you can consider how to arrange your belongings in a way that welcomes the energy that can bring personal, professional, and financial rewards. As you look at the arrangement of your interior spaces, you also want to consider the feng shui principle that the environment should feel like a comfortable place in which to exist as well as coexist and interact with others. You should be able to move freely through the space, feel calm and undistracted, and communication should be easy to foster.

A few additional fundamentals of feng shui to contemplate include:

- Avoid seating arrangements that place peoples' backs toward a door. People are instinctively uncomfortable in this arrangement, as there is a feeling that someone could sneak up behind them.
- Flowing water and moving air stir up positive energy within a home. A small flowing fountain can serve as a water element

in your home, and you should leave ceiling fans on to create moving air currents.

- A desk or work area should never be placed facing a wall. If you work on your finances here the wall will block positive money-making energy. If you pursue creative endeavors, your ideas and imagination will be unable to flow freely if you are facing a wall.

- Place your bed in a position where you can see the door of your bedroom. You want to be able to see anyone or anything entering the area where you are resting. This placement will allow you to sleep more soundly.

- The beautiful thing about feng shui is that you can receive maximum benefits from its practice by both a literal and symbolic representation of its ideas. For example, let's say that the best place to put your desk is facing a window that looks out onto a beautiful scene from nature. Unfortunately, the only window in your fourth-story urban apartment looks out over a traffic-filled street and at the brick building across the street. You can still benefit from the natural laws of feng shui by placing your desk in front of a painting of a beautiful scene from nature.

These are just a few of the most basic principles of feng shui. If you are interested in utilizing this practice to help you arrange and decorate your home, there are great resources available at your local bookstore or library.

As you strive to incorporate the quality of rapture into your everyday life, remember that when all is said and done your memories are not in things—they are in you. The memories that you make today, tomorrow, and far into the future rely more on the qualities that you bring to them: joy, laughter, embracing every life experience. Don't place too high a value on any material possession. Know in your heart that if all your stuff was gone tomorrow, damaged in a fire, or tossed by a tornado, everything you really need to survive and to thrive is placed safely on the shelves of your heart.

TRY THIS

Find three things in your house (if you absolutely have to, you can make it five) that you feel you could not live without—your most prized possessions. Get out your journal and write about the three items. Where did they come from? Why are they so important to you? What do you think of and how does it make you feel when you see them or touch them? Is there anything you can do to better care for or protect these items? Write a story about the day you found this particular piece, or the occasion for which it was given to you, or the circumstances surrounding its acquisition. Maybe take a picture of the item and place it in your journal along with your writing. It will be fun for you to look back on these entries and children or other loved ones will enjoy reflecting on items that you have held dear and the feelings they invoked. What could you do to engage in an experience that might lead to the discovery of another highly prized treasure?

mantra for meditation on possessions

Everything within my home is beautiful, meaningful, or functional.

haiku on stuff

it is just a thing
remember reflect rejoice
that is what is real

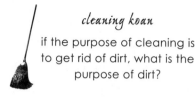

zen concept
reverence for nature

cleaning koan
if the purpose of cleaning is
to get rid of dirt, what is the
purpose of dirt?

EIGHT.

CLEANING GREEN

$\mathcal{P}$erhaps dirt is meant to remind us that we cannot control things no matter how hard we try and that ultimately Mother Nature is much more powerful than we are. Dust is going to accumulate. Spiders are going to spin and create cobwebs. Mud is going to get tracked in and glasses of wine are going to spill. In physics this concept is called *entropy*, a law of nature as real and powerful as gravity, which states that the natural order of things is movement toward disorder. There is a very delicate balance that exists in our universe. As we clean, we are working to impose order on a system, our home, which is naturally going to try to become disorderly. For decades, we have been attempting to impose that order through the use of cleaners that break down dirt through a chemical process. We are only now beginning to realize the impact that process is having on our health, the safety of our homes, and the planet itself.

The Japanese culture that gave rise to Zen has always held nature in high esteem. Nature is revered. It is looked upon as a companion, and throughout Japanese history, human beings and elements of nature have shared a relationship that makes them as interconnected as a close relative, as if the environment were our brother or sister. When you look at planet Earth as if it is a close relative, it makes even more sense to try to do everything humanly possible to sustain it. As you begin to live Zen, one of the great awakenings that will occur is the internalizing of the concept that while you are one perfect individual, you are also a single component of *every other thing* at the same time. Thus, poisoning your home and the planet with an overabundance of toxins is the equivalent of poisoning yourself and the ones that you love. What can you do? Clean green.

Buddha Says . . .
"He who experiences the unity of life sees his own Self in all beings, and all beings in his own Self."

The Environmental Protection Agency conducted a five-year study during which it was determined that the air in the average American home has chemical contamination levels seventy times greater than the air outside. We thought we were opening the windows to let fresh air in, when what we really need to be doing is letting contaminated air out. The main culprit in this contamination? Cleaning products. Across the country, over 32 million pounds of household cleaners are poured down drains each day. Guess who is the number one-violator of chemical waste regulations per capita? The neighborhood nuclear power plant? No. It is the typical American household.

IT'S NOT EASY BEING GREEN!

Well, actually, it's easier than you think. At long last, the vast majority of us have embraced recycling as a part of our lifestyle. It is easy enough to integrate into our daily routine and we are convinced of its necessity. Now we must address the issue of *sustainability*—meeting the needs of present-day people while attempting to ensure that there are adequate resources for future generations to meet theirs and that there is a viable planet on which these future generations can exist. This next wave of earth-friendly approaches to daily living are contained under the umbrella of "living green"—doing as much as you can to reduce the negative impact you have on the earth.

Green-living practices encompass everything from driving a hybrid (or biking or walking wherever you need to go) to buying coffee that is guaranteed to be made from beans picked by well-paid and well-treated bean pickers in Colombia. Of course, if you are going to buy these worker-friendly coffee beans you will most certainly want to percolate them in the unbleached coffee filters! You can purchase foods from the grocery store that aren't treated with environment-polluting chemicals and carry your groceries home from the store in organic cotton bags. Your efforts can be as minor as you wish and feel comfortable with, or you can make a major commitment to living a greener lifestyle and use this opportunity to make truly meaningful changes in the way you live. Either way, a great place to start is in making the transition to green cleaning.

It is surprisingly simple to implement green-cleaning practices. Your goal in green cleaning is to reduce the use of toxic chemicals in your home, not just to save the planet but to save the health of your family as well. Multitudes of current scientific research studies are linking the use of cleaning chemicals and the residues they leave behind on dishes, clothes, and other household surfaces to everything from the rise in infertility to the prevalence of conditions such as asthma and attention deficit disorder in our children. Not to mention the impact on our environment and its ecosystems. Where should you begin to green your cleaning? The answer is as close as the nearest box of baking soda.

THE WORLD'S GREATEST CLEANING PRODUCTS ARE PROBABLY IN YOUR PANTRY RIGHT NOW

We've always known to put a box of baking soda in the back of the refrigerator and freezer to absorb odors, but did you know that baking soda is a natural abrasive and cleanser? It can be used for everything from brushing your teeth to scrubbing your toilets. Other natural cleansing agents are lemon

Zen Homemasters

"I'm struggling to get computer savvy. I basically know how to send and receive e-mail. But one thing I do look to the computer for is information on natural health alternatives and cleaning solutions. This generation is so much more tuned in to protecting their health and the health of the planet and a ton of great information is available on their preferred medium of communication—the computer."

—*Sue Cassel*
Retired medical technologist and mother of two grown children
Austin, Texas

juice, vinegar, and olive oil, which is used to bind these elements together for their greatest impact and to condition cleansed surfaces. If you don't find them effective as cleaning products, just add a little garlic powder and toss them with a salad or drizzle over some whole-grain pasta!

If you aren't the do-it-yourself type, just shop with "green" in mind. Method Home and Seventh Generation are just two of the many companies committed to providing cleaning products that are earth friendly. On the Method Web site they explain that most highly chemicalized cleaners work by breaking down the dirt, whereas Method products absorb it. They are also fragranced with natural oils derived from plants, not perfumed with chemicals that have unpronounceable names. In addition to all types of cleansers for home and body, Seventh Generation has a line of paper products that include chlorine-free diapers and feminine hygiene products. Shaklee has long been well known as a supplier of quality vitamins, and it is one of the first companies

Living One with Nature

The U.S. Department of the Interior, the primary federal agency concerned with conservation and environmental protection issues, has over twenty criteria in place for a cleaning product to be considered green. The top five are:

- Products must be bio-based and from renewable resources, a fruit, vegetable, or plant.
- The cleaner must contain no petro-dyes.
- Cleaners must not contain petro-artificial perfumes.
- The product must be biodegradable.
- The cleaner must not contain any petroleum distillates or crude oil.

to successfully utilize independent consultants to direct-sell to their customers and make a profit from word-of-mouth references. When other companies were jumping on the bandwagon of synthetics and chemical fillers, Shaklee stayed true to its original vision and continued to rely on natural ingredients. In addition to their products promoting personal health, they now have an extensive and well-respected line of cleaning products that are helping ensure the health of the planet.

The companies mentioned here have shown a long-standing commitment to environmental protection. They have been adhering to high standards for packaging and production and using quality natural ingredients for decades. Be aware that there are companies and organizations out there that are not so sincerely committed to the betterment or sustainability of our planet and are just jumping on the "green bandwagon" in order to increase profit margin.

BEWARE OF GREENWASHING

Greenwashing is when a company uses misleading propaganda to make you think they are environmentally conscious when their actual business practices reflect otherwise. A company may tout itself as environmentally friendly when their production plants are still pouring hazardous waste into rivers and streams. The greenwashing technique that you have most likely been exposed to, however, has probably taken place right in your neighborhood grocery store.

OSHA (Occupational Safety and Health Administration) is responsible for the regulation of chemicals that can be used in workplaces, but while guidelines and suggestions are beginning to be implemented for products we use in the home, there is still no regulation on what can be promised on a label. A product can claim it is "natural," "nontoxic," or "environmentally friendly" with little to no substantiation. Your best defense against toxic cleaning products is research and knowledge. Become an avid reader of labels, and if the majority of ingredients are unpronounceable chemicals, put it back on the shelf. Also, if there is not a *complete* list of ingredients, chances are there is something harmful being hidden there. A lot of cleaners will list their active ingredient and then make some ambiguous statement like "98 percent other ingredients." If they can't list them, you don't want them! The more information a label gives, the more likely you can trust what the company says about their product. The Internet is also a great resource for information on every aspect of green living, specifically eco-friendly products and the companies that make them.

Buddha Says . . .
"Believe nothing, no matter where you read it, or who said it, no matter if I have said it, unless it agrees with your own reason and your own common sense."

Some other ingredients often found in household cleaning products to be on the lookout for:

- Artificial colors—many have long been known to be carcinogenic.

- Artificial fragrances—synthesized chemicals created to make products sweet smelling can set off a migraine, trigger allergies, and aggravate asthma. And those are just the side effects that we know of!

- APEs (alkylphenol ethoxylates)—these are contained in many inexpensive cleaners, and when they break down they impact our endocrine system—the incredibly intricate system that is responsible for metabolism, hormone production, and reproductive health. It is believed that exposure to these APEs may be a large contributor to increased infertility rates and low sperm counts.

- Laundry detergents—these products can contain many harmful chemicals or create dangerous by-products. Optical brighteners are far more dangerous than they sound. OBs are petroleum based and are particularly harmful to aquatic life when they enter rivers and streams after they drain from your washing machine. If you or a loved one experiences an allergic reaction to a laundry detergent, chances are you are reacting to the presence of one of these OBs.

- Benzene—this is another ingredient proven to be a human carcinogen, which is often found in laundry soap.

If that's not enough to steer you clear of many of today's cleaning products, consider this: Scientists are concerned that our use of chemically produced antimicrobial and antibacterial products such as the pesticide triclosan (yep, you read that right—many of the products you use to clean your home each day contain a pesticide!) is helping to hasten the proliferation of "superbugs." Germs are becoming more and more resistant to our cleaning efforts and studies have shown that use of these agents is really no more effective than washing with simple soap and water. The overprescribing of antibiotics, primarily for our children, is having the same effect on human health. More and more illnesses are becoming untreatable because of their resistance to the drugs we are using to treat them.

Awareness of the impact you are having on the planet and its people, primarily the people in your little corner of the world, your home, can be a meaningful step on your Zen journey.

OTHER WAYS YOU CAN
GREEN WHILE YOU CLEAN

Using natural products is but one facet of cleaning green. Look for products that are recycled or recyclable, detergents that are biodegradable, and products that have limited packaging. Think products such as these would be hard to find or expensive? Major corporations and producers of cleaning products such as Procter & Gamble are implementing plans to reduce packaging by selling more-concentrated dishwashing liquid. The mega-giant Wal-Mart is making an effort to get green on a variety of fronts. They are going to such lengths as putting skylights in the ceilings of newly constructed stores in order to use less energy. They are also changing to energy-efficient light bulbs in their already-existing facilities. Wal-Mart products are also receiving packaging makeovers to create less waste and therefore less impact on the environment. The price point for these products will be similar to current products of the same quality. While there *are* people at the top levels of management of these corporations who have the best interest of Mother Earth in mind, it *is* business, and business is about the bottom line. Companies have found that going green both *makes* them more green and practicing conservation *saves* them green. It can do the same for you!

Green cleaning is good for the planet. It is good for your health and the health of your family. It's also good for *your* bottom line. Green cleaning, particularly if you try the easy-to-follow recipes for mixing up your own cleaning products, is less expensive than purchasing regular cleaning products that may be toxic to the planet and to your home.

More Reasons to Green While You Clean

Do you need more incentive to start cleaning green? Okay, how about this? Doing laundry less often is kinder to the environment, as is washing dishes less frequently! Even when you set your washing machine or dishwasher for a small load, the amount of water consumed is enormous. Just wait until you have an entire load. And if it isn't really dirty, don't wash it. It

Seeds of Rapture

Implementing green living practices sets an excellent example for your children. The planet will most likely be fine for the course of our lifetime, so you must remember that much of the greening you are embracing is for future generations. Leading by example will ensure that they are stewards of the planet for themselves and for their descendants.

can be worn again. Towels do *not* have to be washed after every single use. If they are hung up to dry instead of thrown in a pile on the floor, they can make it for a couple of additional uses. The same goes for clothes that need to be dry-cleaned. Don't take them to the dry cleaner after every wearing. Dry cleaners are making strides to be more environmentally friendly, but the processes that the majority of dry cleaners use release a toxic substance known as perchloroethylene. Help minimize its impact on the planet by dry-cleaning less and washing and ironing more at home.

Last but not least, use common sense when it comes to your use of resources. When you wash your dishes (or your face or brush your teeth), turn the water off while you are scrubbing. Turn lights off when not in use. Set your thermostat at reasonable temperatures and use your fans. Make a list of errands that need to be run and then organize them in a way that will minimize the driving you have to do. This will save gas and another incredibly valuable resource that can't be renewed: time.

THE HOME IN YOUR HEAD—
MAKE IT "GREEN" TOO!

One of the unexpected advantages of having a child involved in sports is that every season you get to meet a whole new batch of great kids and their great parents. This baseball season was no exception. As our sons learned more about the great American pastime, baseball, I got to know one mom particularly well. Patti Mandrell is a professional mental health counselor here in Lubbock, Texas, and one of the leading experts in the world in the field of equine-assisted psychotherapy, utilizing horses for maximizing the mental health of her clients. She and her husband work together at their stables, she conducting therapy and he training the horses. They also provide training for people nationwide who are pursuing equine therapy certification.

One evening, we began discussing housework. She said she often uses the home as an analogy in working with her clients. The way you care for your home and the way you care for your health, both mental and physical, are either very similar or at great odds with each other, depending on how integrated different aspects of your personality are. Her words reminded me of those of English writer Rumer Godden, who said that we are all houses made up of four rooms, physical, mental, emotional, and spiritual. We usually live in one room of our "house" most of the time, but in order to fully realize our human potential, we must go into each room, every day, even if just to "keep it aired."

Patti says she emphasizes to her clients the importance of getting back to basics—in all areas of life. I told her about my research on cleaning green and asked for her thoughts. After an entire evening's baseball practice discussing it, we concluded that the chemicals, fragrances, and dyes found in most cleaning products can actually come between you and your ultimate goal: a clean home. You think you need a multitude of specialized products, different fragrances for different rooms of the house, a different spray for every surface. Do you really need all that extra stuff? This same thinking can and should be applied to your efforts to declutter your home and to declutter your head with your meditation and mindfulness. When you get back to basics it is much easier to see your ultimate goal and to get there with less interference.

HERE'S TO YOUR HEALTH—GREENING, CLEANING, AND LIVING CLUTTER-FREE

I am by no means a professional cleaning expert, nor am I a practicing Buddhist. I'm just one woman trying to find the path that works for me and the best combination of practices to help me get there, and to then share them with you. Another thing I am not is a medical professional. What I do know, however, is that living a complicated, cluttered, and convoluted life took a toll on my health—both physical and emotional.

A myriad of strange and seemingly unrelated symptoms had me frequently at the doctor's office and on a first-name basis with my pharmacist. I was able to treat most of the symptoms but was unable to discover the cause or a cure. I am still a relatively young woman (not even forty yet!) and I had always been the picture of good health, but over time I began to feel like I was falling apart or getting older by the minute, and neither one were acceptable options to me. My hands were dry and scaly and would often crack and bleed. My joints and muscles ached without explanation and I had recurring bouts with depression and anxiety. Plus, no matter how much sleep I was getting or coffee I was drinking, I always felt tired.

Recently, a persistent practitioner discovered that all these symptoms were indeed connected and easily remedied. I was suffering from an underactive thyroid.

What does this have to with green living or with cleaning? Everything! My diagnosis motivated me to read everything I could about this and related conditions. Why did I have this? How could it best be treated? Where did it come from? In my case, a small dose of synthetic thyroid was all that was necessary to get me back on track. So what had happened to throw me so out of whack?

The thyroid is a tiny gland at the base of your throat that has a huge job: It regulates your metabolism. It works in conjunction with your pituitary, adrenal glands, and other elements of the extremely complex endocrine system. This endocrine system regulates a multitude of functions in your body—energy levels, ability to concentrate, the release and regulation of hormones. My research made it abundantly clear that this system is extremely sensitive to external stressors. The incidence of underactive thyroid is becoming epidemic in its scope and scientists are hypothesizing and building bodies of research to support the conclusion that one of the major causes of this ailment is our regular exposure to toxic chemicals—in the air we breath, the water we drink, the food we eat, and in the products we use to clean our homes. Our bodies were never intended to process this many chemicals and they are struggling to keep up, but for many of us, it is just more work than our bodies can bear.

Yes, the current living green buzzword is *sustainability*—actively sustaining the health of our planet. If we are not sustaining our own health, however, and the health of our families, what difference is a healthier planet really going to make? It may take a little time to break the habit of reaching for the quickest and most convenient cleaning product on the grocery store shelves and learning to use natural products and cleansers. It may be a bit more expensive to buy organic fruits and vegetables that are grown without the use of pesticides. You may have to go out of your way to find chicken or beef that is hormone free. But aren't you worth it?

Another modern-day malady that is sapping our health and vitality is adrenal fatigue. The adrenal glands, part of that amazing endocrine system, produce and distribute adrenaline throughout your body in times of stress. Adrenaline is responsible for our fight-or-flight response, either giving us the guts and strength to fight for our safety and well-being

Buddha Says . . .

"No one saves us but ourselves. No one can and no one may. We ourselves must walk the path."

or the energy to run in the opposite direction—fast! A high level of adrenaline is not supposed to be a constant in our bodies; it is supposed to be reserved for genuine stress. When we exist, unrelentingly, under enormous stress, as the vast majority of us do in today's world, our adrenal glands simply get worn out from having to produce adrenaline all the time. We are left feeling like we have no get-up-and-go, even when we need it. So we guzzle coffee, smoke cigarettes, or engage in other unhealthy habits just to try to get the boost we need.

Life today is, by the very nature of the world in which we live, inherently stressful. We are constantly bombarded by news of war, poverty, and turmoil. We are able to be in constant contact—with everyone—never able to engage in a moment of peace and quiet. We are overworked, overscheduled, and filling our bodies full of overprocessed foods and overtly harmful toxins. Add to this our use of chemicals to clean our homes and it is little wonder that we don't feel good. What else adds stress to our already intense lives? A dirty and disorganized home. We have no place to go to escape from the outside world. And when we are in the midst of the disarray, it only serves to heighten our anxiety and levels of stress.

OTHER HOUSEHOLD HEALTH ISSUES

It is not just *your* mental and physical health that may be impacted by your cleaning practices. Houses that are poorly maintained can cause a multitude of health problems for its occupants.

A commitment to more extensive cleaning won't guarantee that your children will never get another cold or that your spouse will be the picture of perfect health, but there are steps you can take to minimize environmental hazards to the health of your loved ones.

The cause of asthma and other respiratory conditions are in large part a mystery, but experts are certain that triggers in the environment such as dust, mold, and cigarette smoke can trigger attacks. Keeping carpets cleaned and vacuumed, air filters changed regularly, vents vacuumed, and all surfaces free from mold will make for easier breathing in your home. Bedding should also be changed at least once a week. These materials can harbor germs and are also favored places for dust mites to reside. Dust mites are a major irritant to many biological systems and can cause allergic reactions of the respiratory system and the skin.

The greatest hazard to our health and the one that can be most easily defeated through good cleaning practices is the common germ. Wipe down all surfaces regularly with an antibacterial solution. Trade out toothbrushes periodically (immediately if someone gets sick). Wash your children's toys regularly. You can run most plastic toys through a gentle dishwasher cycle and most stuffed animals do just fine taking a trip through the washer and dryer on occasion. Don't forget to clean the toys that your kids play with in the bathtub. Just because they are in the tub with the children does not ensure that they are clean. Stagnant water can be a breeding ground for germs. Rinse bath toys and let them dry completely after each use.

A lot of illness prevention is simple common sense, but a reminder doesn't hurt. Just a few extra minutes a day can ensure a lot fewer trips to the doctor's office.

SUSTAINING GOOD HEALTH

What's the answer to improving your health and that of your family? An across-the-board, back-to-basics approach to living. Utilize the calming powers of Zen that we have discussed here and use their practice to motivate you to once and for all get down to the basics. Simplify the products you use to clean, and follow your system to accomplish each task in a timely and efficient manner. Minimize the toxins that are in your home, both in the products you use and the food that you eat. Breathe deeply. Live fully in each moment. Eat well. Sleep. Walk. Love. Live.

Chances are you will never have to deal with the major health issues I've discussed here and that you've already addressed the minor ones. But researching them raised my awareness and reinforced to me the importance of my Zen journey—and letting it expand into all areas of my life. I not only feel better, but I'm also doing good things for the planet and improving the health and quality of life of my husband and children. *That* is sustainability in action!

Seeds of Rapture

Giving green gifts gives twice—once to the recipient and again to the long-term sustainability of the planet.

- Consider buying a friend a tree from Gift of Green. A tree will be planted in the depleted Kootenai National Forest in Montana.
- Buy a star and name it after a friend.
- Give an organic gardening kit complete with seeds and instructions for starting your own organic vegetable or flower garden.
- Instead of giving a gift, give someone the gift of your time by taking them to lunch.
- Give gift certificates to a local nursery or health food store.
- Search out clothing made from recycled materials. These items are becoming much more readily available.
- Buy tickets to a concert or art exhibit.

GIVE GREEN GIFTS

As you are clearing your life of clutter, you don't want to contribute to clutter in someone else's home. Green gifts can be unique, thoughtful, and also help spread the word about the importance of greening.

TRY THIS

Get back to nature. Find something in nature that moves you. That speaks to you. That inspires or never ceases to amaze you. It can be anything. Snowflakes hitting the ground. Squirrels burying nuts. A moon or sunrise. A patch of wildflowers. Something that no matter how often you see it never fails to make you stop for a minute and say, "Wow!" Take five minutes at least, all alone, and just observe your chosen wonder. Spend more time if you can possibly spare it or repeat this exercise as often as you can. It will ground you and help you regain your perspective unlike any other exercise. Let your mind ponder your chosen natural occurrence. Let your thoughts go wherever they want to go without censorship from you. What does it make you think of? How does it make you feel? Does it remind you of something or someone? Stay with this "moment" as long as you can or as long as you can do it in solitude. Reserve time just for you to experience this wonder, but also consider sharing it with friends or your children. It's a great way to get little ones thinking about nature and how they feel about it. It takes your mind off of you and puts it onto something that is much bigger. As you and the members of your family grow in your mindful appreciation of nature, it will become even easier to embrace the practice of living and cleaning green.

mantra for meditation on cleaning green

I will strive to do no harm to this planet or to those who dwell on it.

green haiku

treating this planet
as a friend and a lover
with utmost respect

NINE.

CLEANING WITH THE SEASONS

*W*hen you first began to develop your housekeeping system, the main area of concern was defining and gaining control over the tasks that had to be performed on a weekly basis. It is now time to revisit your system and incorporate longer-range projects, those that need to be performed monthly and semiannually. Difficult tasks are always more fun if performed with a friend, so I encourage you to enlist the help of Mother Nature in this process. She can be an invaluable partner by giving you extremely obvious reminders that it is time to tackle these bigger tasks. She offers these clues to us and provides us with the answer to this chapter's cleaning koan, "What gives life its flavor?" The seasons!

THE FOUR SEASONS

The Italian composer Vivaldi came as close as anyone to capturing the magic and power of the seasons when he created the violin concertos *The Four Seasons* in the late 1700s. Each concerto captures the sounds and the feeling of the seasons. However, nothing can compare to fully experiencing the wonder of changing seasons for yourself.

The changing of the seasons is one of the most amazing and impactful natural occurrences, and it has guided homemakers throughout history. Having grown up in the South, I was unaware of the power of the visual clues offered by the changing seasons, like the intense and rich colors of fall to be found further north, until we moved to Pennsylvania. Prior to that time, I also had no appreciation or understanding of the calm and quiet of new-fallen snow. Nor did I know the joy or anticipation of spring's first buds after a long bleak winter.

Growing up in Texas, we had hot, really hot, hotter than hell, and football season. Yes, four seasons, but not quite as awe-inspiring as the four seasons nature had to offer when we lived in the northeast. The time we spent in Louisiana exposed me to another way of looking at the seasons. In Cajun country, the seasons were based on the type of seafood that was freshest. You had shrimp season, crawfish season, crab season, and

Buddha Says . . .
"The secret of health for both mind and body is not to mourn for the past, worry about the future, or anticipate troubles, but to live in the present moment wisely and earnestly."

oyster season. Whatever seasons you experience where you live, honor their passing and use them as indicators that it is time to engage in some extensive home maintenance projects.

MAYDAY, MAYDAY!

Celebrated on May first, the May Day holiday dates back to pre-Christian religious observances of the arrival of summer. For our purposes, it is our reminder that on the first of every month, there are certain household maintenance duties that need to be performed.

On the first of each month:

- Change your air filters.
- Vacuum air vents and ceiling fans.
- Replace any burned-out light bulbs that haven't already been replaced.
- Thoroughly clean out the refrigerator and pantry.
- Clean inside of all windows.
- Dust all surfaces of electronic equipment.
- Do a quick inventory of all closets. Is there an item that you have decided you will never wear again? Have the kids outgrown anything? Get unnecessary items to Goodwill.
- Is there mending that you have been putting off? Gather it together and get it done while watching a good movie or talking on the phone to a faraway friend.

Monthly maintenance should keep your house and its contents running smoothly between bigger household maintenance jobs that should be completed with the changing of the seasons. Fall and spring are the two seasons that require that we make and master seasonal "to do" lists. Take full advantage of these interim seasons when the weather is mild and your anticipation of the season ahead spurs you to action.

SPRING FORWARD

The changing of the clocks from daylight savings to standard time and back again is an arbitrary dividing line in our celebration of the seasons. But it does make sense to connect as many processes as you possibly can to the time change. It is a simple reminder and you can always be certain of the last time that you did these tasks. In both spring and fall:

- Change your fire alarm batteries.
- Check that all smoke and carbon monoxide monitors are working properly.
- Check the pressure on fire extinguishers.
- Vacuum refrigerator coils.
- Power-wash home exteriors.
- Clean windows inside and out.

When the first blooms appear on the trees and a warm breeze begins to blow, it is surely a sign that it is time for spring cleaning.

While I'm sure women throughout history have always welcomed spring and the opportunity to open doors and windows and move back into the outside world, the annual housekeeping rite of passage that we practice today can trace its roots back to the early 1800s and the industrial revolution. At that time, poet Emily Dickinson once said of spring cleaning, "House is being cleaned. I prefer pestilence." Emily Dickinson didn't hate housekeeping per se. In fact, she was a notorious homebody, isolating herself in her home to the point that many biographers feel she may have suffered from agoraphobia. What she hated was the despicably dirty job that was the precursor of today's spring-cleaning ritual. When the fuels that were used to heat our homes were the notorious soot producers coal, oil, and wood, every single surface inside houses, particularly in colder climates, were covered in thick black soot after a winter of closed windows and heating. The process of "spring cleaning" a home was a dreaded task.

Buddha Says . . .

"Peace comes from within. Do not seek it without."

For modern homemakers, spring cleaning should be seen as a celebration of renewal and an opportunity to prepare for the seasons ahead. Tasks to include on your Spring Cleaning Checklist should include:

- Making an appointment to have your air conditioner serviced. Don't wait until the schedule of the best local heating and cooling company is full and the mercury is rising above 90 to discover there's a problem with your cooling system.

- Get outdoor furniture out of storage and clean it.
- Rotate the clothes in everyone's closets. Bring warm-weather clothes out of storage or to the front of the closet and prepare, pack, and put cold-weather clothes away or in the back of the closet.
- Do a close inspection of the outside perimeter of your home. Note any projects that need to be undertaken, whether they are repairs to the roof, plumbing updates, or lawn and landscape issues and make appointments for these things to be taken care of before the official arrival of summer.
- Drain and clean the pan underneath your water heater. Sediment settles there and needs to be removed for maximum efficiency.
- Review your skin and hair care supplies and make lists of any items that you need to purchase. Remember that warmer weather will call for different skin and hair care products like conditioners for your hair after swimming and sunscreen for all members of the family.
- Warmer weather also calls for lighter makeup and brighter colors. Go get a makeover in celebration of the season.

FALL BACK

I have always thought fall was very festive. My birthday is in the fall, I am a huge fan of football and Halloween, and cooler weather lifts my spirits and infuses me with energy. It also feels like a season brimming with anticipation as we lead up to the holidays, the most fun-filled

Seeds of Rapture

Throw a party to celebrate the changing of the seasons. Many of our holidays have evolved from pagan celebrations of occurrences like the summer solstice or the arrival of the autumnal equinox. Why not revive some of these traditions and begin an annual ritual of celebrating the seasons as they change?

time of the year. By developing and executing a really comprehensive fall home-maintenance checklist, you can not only be prepared for the harsh winter that may lie ahead, but you can also get a jump on holiday preparations that will leave you cool, calm, and collected while everyone else fights for a parking place at the mall.

Your Fall Checklist should include the following:

- Rotate clothes again—warm-weather ones to the back or to storage, cold-weather ones unpacked and moved to the front.
- Have a checkup done for your heating system.
- Clean the fireplace and chimney.
- Check the weather stripping on windows and doors and replace it if necessary.
- Wash outside windows.
- Prepare outdoor pipes for harsh weather if you live in an extremely cold environment.
- Clean and store all outdoor furniture.
- Flip all mattresses front to back and one end to the other if the types of mattresses you own suggest this type of maintenance. (Many of today's pillow-tops require only end to end rotation or no rotation at all. For regular mattresses, however, this

annual maintenance increases the length of their life and the quality of sleep you will receive.)

- Launch a full-scale declutter session in your kitchen, particularly if you like to do a lot of baking during the holidays.
- Inspect the backs of your washer and dryer to make sure there is no buildup of dust or lint behind them (fire hazard!) and that all hoses and connections are in good working order and securely fastened.

The Spring and Fall Cleaning Checklists provided here are by no means all-inclusive, but they give you an idea of the types of projects that are necessary to keep your house running smoothly. Men, even ones that don't do much of the regular household maintenance, enjoy getting involved with some of these bigger projects around the house. Make these seasonal cleaning sessions family affairs. Get everyone involved. With the big jobs behind you and your home having received its regular six-month checkup, you and yours can more fully appreciate the joy that comes with the changing of the seasons.

MAKING THE MOST OF WINTER AND SUMMER

Each of the four seasons has its own distinct character. Summer is for fun, relaxation, vacations. Life goes at a slightly slower pace. Kids are out of school. The rising temperature makes you long for a nap in the comfort of the air-conditioned house or encourages you to seek out a shady spot under a tree or a blanket on the beach where you can read a trashy romance novel. Household maintenance is the last thing on your mind.

In winter, everything and everyone turn inward. We sit close to the fire, we simmer pots of stew on the stove, and we layer ourselves in hats, scarves, and mittens before we venture outdoors. This is not the time either to engage in large internal *or* external maintenance projects, but that doesn't mean you are off the hook for housekeeping during these seasons.

Certainly you must maintain your weekly cleaning schedule and monthly maintenance duties regardless of the time of year. With winter's arrival, however, you must be even more vigilant than normal about ridding your home of germs that can cause colds and flu (among other unwanted illnesses). Lysol (or another antibacterial product) should become a constant companion when you are keeping house. Remember to spray and wipe down places you would not normally think of—telephone receivers, doorknobs, computer keyboards.

Remind the members of your household to wash their hands frequently. Antibacterial soap is not necessary. In fact, studies are now showing that regular soap and water is more effective in killing germs anyway, and the overuse of antibacterial products may actually create "superbugs," germs that become resistant to our best efforts to kill them. With the extreme weather outside and the constant heat inside, you may also want to put a bottle of mild, pure hand lotion by each sink. After washing, everybody can moisturize and hopefully reduce the incidence of dry, chapped skin.

If you live in a place that really gets hit with winter weather, it may be your floors that need the most maintenance in your winter housekeeping routine. Wet and muddy boots and shoes, jackets dripping with snow, and a multitude of gloves and scarves can make for a really big mess. If you are fortunate enough to have a mudroom in your house, you have a place for all those wet and woolly cold weather necessities to go. If not, get a big plastic bin in which everyone can put their gear as soon as they come in the door. Also invest in some heavy-duty all-weather doormats so you can wipe your feet as soon as you come inside. This will save you a lot of mopping and also prevent you from having to remove mud stains from your carpet.

In the summertime, it is usually the amount of laundry that becomes daunting. In a perfect world, you and yours are often outside during these hotter months and your house stays a bit more orderly. But it is not a perfect world. With everyone getting hot and sweaty, you often change clothes several times a day. Swimming and showers ensure that there will be lots of towels in need of washing.

If you have children, summertime is a good time to work with them on helping out around the house. Let them collect laundry and pick up their rooms before they can go out with friends. Enlist their services with yard work, gardening, and other outdoor tasks. Mostly, though, summer should be a time for fun. It is more important now than ever that you stick to your schedule and leave plenty of time to enjoy life!

Try making summer a time for planning what big home improvement projects you will tackle when fall arrives. Read decorating magazines, visit paint stores, look at your home inside and out with a critical eye. What would improve its curb appeal or make it more livable or lovable? Summer is a good time for dreaming. You can worry about the doing later!

THE ELEMENTS AND THEIR IMPACT ON CLEANING

In addition to the four seasons, we can also look to the four basic elements found in nature to guide our cleaning efforts. Consider these lines from the classic Zen text *The Sandokai*:

The Four Elements return to their natures,
Just as a child turns to its mother.

Fire heats, wind moves,
Water wets, earth is solid.

Eye and sights, ear and sounds,
Nose and smells, tongue and tastes;

Thus for each and every thing,
According to the roots, the leaves spread forth.

As we clean our homes, we are tapping into and attempting to harness the power of the four elements to assist us in cleaning our homes. We enlist all of our senses in ensuring that things are done right. Allow yourself to be reminded of the powerful forces that are on your side as you clean your home and never forget that the purpose behind the work you are doing is for yourself and your loved ones to have solid earth in which to plant your roots so that the full beauty of your leaves can spread forth.

TRY THIS

Go to your local music store and buy a copy of Vivaldi's *Four Seasons*. Bring it home, put it in the CD player, light a few candles, pour yourself a drink, and sit down with your housekeeping journal. As you listen to the beautiful music, consider ways in which you can take more full advantage of the changing of the seasons to maintain your house, and put those ideas down on paper. What rituals do you and your family enjoy that need to be included in your monthly or seasonal routines? What times of the year are most stressful at your house and why? What can you do to make these times of the year go more smoothly? Are you really celebrating the seasons and giving their arrival the attention they deserve? The flavor of each season of the year is rich and unique. Honoring them will make you feel far more in tune with the world around you.

mantra for meditating with mother nature

Mother Nature, guide me so that i may work in a way that honors your strength, grace, and beauty.

haiku to the four seasons

winter and summer
my companions in cleaning
spring and fall always

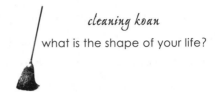

TEN.

ACHIEVING ENLIGHTENMENT

*F*or any practitioner of Zen, the goal is continuous movement toward enlightenment. As a Zen Homemaster, our enlightenment is to be found within the walls of our homes. We will know we are well on our way by the newfound calm that replaces our harried and hassled way of life. We will no longer resist what needs to be done within our homes but will value the worth of the work that we do there and embrace the opportunity to contemplate the meaning of our life as it relates to each precious moment. All activities, both large and small, will build on each other until they have created a significant accomplishment—a home that runs smoothly and fosters the growth of all who dwell there.

You have contemplated the barriers that stand between you and the home and housekeeping standards that you want to embrace. You have developed a system that when followed will give you a concrete beginning and end to the work you do in your home and a framework around which to prioritize the other important elements of your life. You have decluttered every room of your home and learned how to apply time-tested tricks and tools of the trade to your housekeeping. Most importantly, you have been reminded of the importance of honoring your own intrinsic worth and the worth of those that surround you. With your home in order, you are now ready to explore how to bring meaning and beauty back into your home and your life. Your home can become your *zendo*.

A zendo is a Zen meditation hall where you can go to engage in zazen or kinhin, take a course on Zen, or attend a seminar with other like-minded individuals. It is a place where you can totally immerse yourself in your quest for peace and enlightenment. If you have put into practice all, or even most, of the suggestions and ideas contained within these pages, your home is now well on its way to becoming a place like that for you. However, there is still one very important thing left for us to do: determine the shape of our lives.

The shape of your life is not determined by the exalted moments of magnificent, recognized accomplishment. The shape of your life is defined by the way you live every single day, each individual moment. One of the best ways to honor life's moments is to create rituals around your daily routines and elevate the ordinary to an art form. The Japanese are masters of maximizing the mundane, and examining a few of their practices can give us a starting point for creating our own enriching activities. Developing new rituals, routines, hobbies, and habits that honor your new

Zen approach to keeping house will seem a natural extension of the work that you have already accomplished. Let's explore these artistic expressions of Zen philosophy and create some expressions of our own.

THE ZEN GARDEN

A Zen garden is completely different from gardens as we think of them in the Western world. While we strive for color, fragrance, and often a large variety of plants growing in one place, the Zen garden is made up primarily of monochromatic rocks or stones placed strategically in a bed of gravel. One must eliminate all distractions in order to focus on the essence of the garden. There may be a few plants and decorative accessories in a Zen garden, but while our primary purpose in planting a flower garden is to have something beautiful to look at, every single element in the Zen garden will have a meaning or serve as a symbolic representation of something else. For example, the large stones may be representative of the group of islands that make up the country of Japan, while the gravel is the symbolic sea in which they reside. Islands are believed to be sacred and unreachable by humans; therefore, you will never see bridges built in this type of garden. In other types of Zen gardens, a large stone may represent the mythical mountaintop on which Buddha was believed to have lived. Often the stones are buried with only the top half of the stone visible to encourage the observer to contemplate *miegakure*, the idea that just because you can't see a portion of something it doesn't take away from the whole identity of the object.

Pine trees are often found in the Zen rock garden and symbolize a long and happy life. Plum trees are the first trees to bloom after cold Japanese winters and are often found in the gardens as symbols of strength and vigor. Regardless of the symbolic concept expressed there, the beauty of a Japanese garden is not to be found in its design but rather in the philosophical or spiritual feelings it creates in those who view it and in the gardener who created it.

How can we bring these philosophical and spiritual representations into our own gardens? You probably don't have the space or the desire to create a traditional Zen rock garden, but that doesn't mean that you can't translate the lessons into your own yard or indoor plant-growing practices.

- For the Japanese it is lack of color and sweet smells for which they strive. That is not our aesthetic, and we must be true to ourselves and value what is beautiful to us. Celebrate the colors and fragrances that are present in your yard. Examine and contemplate how many different shades of green there are.
- Look for items to place in your garden that represent each member of your family.
- When you go for a walk, look for interesting rocks that you can incorporate into a potted plant. They can represent absolutely anything that is meaningful to you.
- Pick some outdoor plants to not prune this spring. Let nature take its course and see what happens.

● Use only environmentally friendly fertilizers and bug sprays.

● Consider creating and caring for an indoor herb garden. Utilizing fresh herbs in your cooking elevates the entire experience. Plus it brings a bit of the outside world in.

● If you are growing a vegetable garden, commit to keeping it organic as well.

JAPANESE FLOWER ARRANGING

Some of the principles that hold true in the design of a rock garden are also found in the art of Japanese flower arranging, or *ikebana*, which translates as "flowers kept alive." Two of these qualities are asymmetry and naturalness (*shizen*). Oftentimes our flower arrangements strive for fullness, variety, and a round quality. Japanese flower arrangements are far more linear in their structure. Japanese arrangements have three primary points of focus that symbolize heaven, earth, and humans. Flower arrangements are not just for decoration; they are to be contemplated and considered.

Can we take an opportunity to contemplate and consider flowers in our own daily routine?

● If you have flowers growing in your yard, clip a handful and place them loosely in a simple vase. Don't try to make them look any certain way. Just let them fall where they may and see what their arrangement or lack of arrangement makes you think of. Perhaps you could get out your housekeeping journal and try to sketch the arrangement or write a haiku about the moment in which you find yourself.

- If you aren't a gardener, make the purchasing of fresh flowers a treat you give yourself regularly. Place small bouquets in highly visible places or in places where they might not be expected—like your children's bathrooms. It will cause them to stop for a moment and wonder what they are doing there. That one moment of contemplation can help calm and quiet them. Perhaps they will come to you and ask you about the flowers, opening up a conversation about the importance of nature and bringing beauty into our lives. Zen parenting in action!

- Put fresh-cut flowers on your dining table whenever you serve a meal there. It makes any meal feel just a little more special.

THE TEA CEREMONY

Preparing for, serving, and drinking tea in a traditional tea ceremony is arguably the most important ritual in Japanese culture. It can take up to four hours to participate in a traditional Zen tea ceremony. It is complete with food, appreciation for the art of the room, the flower arrangements, and the dishes used to serve the tea. The utmost attention is given to every single detail. When you enter the room where tea is being served, you symbolically leave cares and worries from the outside world at the door and enter into a spiritual realm. You also leave behind status and social standing. All are considered equal in a tea ceremony. The tea ceremony and the extensive preparations that are made for it pay homage to the uniqueness of each individual guest and recognize that the moments that will occur during the ceremony will never occur again. It is an opportunity to embrace a moment in time that can never be repeated. The ceremony brings together four important principles and puts them into action. They are harmony (with nature and with one another), respect for everyone that is in attendance, purity (cleansing of your mind and spirit), and tranquility.

What would it look like if you gave this kind of attention to a weekly dinner for your family? We live in a world full of activities and outside commitments. Many of us are far too busy to cook our own meals, let alone sit down to dinner together. And yet most experts on the dynamics of family say that the best way to restore some sanity to our lives and relationships is to sit down at the table (and *not* the coffee table all watching the same program on TV) and reconnect. It is probably unrealistic to think that you can possibly make this happen all or even most nights of the week. But is it possible that you can do it one night a week and make it a moment of time that is so special to you and yours that no one would dream of missing it?

Buddha Says . . .
"Thousands of candles can be lighted from a single candle, and the life of the candle will not be shortened. Happiness never decreases by being shared."

- Make a meal (or pick one up—we must remain realistic in our expectations of ourselves) that everyone in the family enjoys.

- Put down a richly colored tablecloth and use cloth napkins.
- Use your good china and silver if you have it. Drink iced tea, water, or milk out of your crystal glasses. We spend far too much time in our life putting off using "the good stuff" for some special occasion that may or may not ever come. *Today* is a special occasion. This moment! Celebrate it.
- Have fresh flowers on the table and light candles.
- Play soft music in the background.

What would this type of weekly gathering do for the ones you love? Would it make them feel as if they are honored and appreciated in your home? Would you?

CREATIVELY CREATING A HOME

Most any artist or creative person, regardless of the art form they engage in, be it music, dance, painting, scrapbooking, writing, or sculpting, will tell you that proper preparation is just as important as the creative act itself. You have to prepare a canvas to receive paint. You have to stretch your muscles and learn the choreography in order to dance. You have to gather all the proper materials, dedicate the time, and be in the right mindset to begin the act of creation. Very few artists engage in their crafts in order to create a perfect piece of art. They do it because they enjoy the process. Creating something out of nothing or beauty where there is a blank slate is deeply satisfying. Engaging in the rituals of reverence for the everyday moment that we have discussed here and making it a priority to create your own should feel like a work of art that you are lovingly creating. Approaching the work in our homes with an artist's eye will take the process to an entirely new level. You are preparing the canvas to create the masterpiece of your life.

WHAT MAKES A HOUSE A HOME?

There is a difference. Most people have a shelter in which they live their daily lives. But a home? That is a different matter altogether. It's a feeling, a place of comfort, an island in this world that protects and nurtures those who dwell there. It is what we are all striving to create, and we must keep that vision crystal clear in our minds. It is up to each of us to determine what makes our house our home. A home is an ever-evolving and always-changing thing. It grows as you grow. It becomes a home as you make memories within its walls. Keep your house clean and celebrate each day and don't worry so much if it is completely picked up at all times. A bit of a mess is the sign that a happy, active family dwells within the walls. A true home will always show signs of life and activity. Its occupants will be engaged in the activities they enjoy, something will be cooking, someone will be singing, a fort will be being built out of blankets and dining-room chairs. When I see a child's bike lying haphazardly in someone's front yard, I always assume something fun is going on inside. A true home is not necessarily pristine. It is a place to play and laugh and experience life. If you allow yourself to become obsessed with keeping your house clean, you may find you are too busy to enjoy the people in it.

BLUE M&M'S

When you don't feel like you can possibly fold one more towel or mop one more floor, when the joy of implementing your rituals escapes you, think of the survivors of tragedies like Hurricane Katrina who would love to have the luxury of having a floor to mop. In her role as the Coordinator for Rural Voices Radio, Emily Noble travels the state of Mississippi and assists children in developing stories that they have written, coaches them on presentation, and then records their stories for broadcast on a statewide radio broadcast. Emily had the opportunity to travel to the Mississippi Gulf Coast just prior to Christmas the year that Hurricane Katrina hit the area. While New Orleans received the lion's share of media coverage, the Mississippi Coast was also devastated by the storm. Emily visited a classroom where the children were building gingerbread houses. And they kept running out of blue M&M's. Many of the children were living in homes (or in trailers next to their homes) where FEMA-distributed blue tarps were serving as roofs. The children were reflecting in their Christmas craft project the lives that they were living, and many of their roofs were blue, thus the utilization of every blue M&M the teachers could find. Emily was extremely moved by the experience, not because the children had lost so much, but because they so fully embraced their present living conditions. They were living in the moment and at that moment their roofs were blue. But just because their roofs were blue didn't mean the places were no longer home. The sense of home could not be swept away by water or blown away by wind.

It was within each child and family, regardless of the color of their roof.

WOMAN'S SEARCH FOR MEANING

Through all of the advances that women have made throughout history—gaining the right to vote, the advent of feminism, breaking the glass ceiling, and so on—we have continued to search for meaning in our own lives, in the work that we do each day and in our lives in their entirety. What is our purpose? What will truly fulfill us? And no matter how far we have come (and we have come a long way, baby), our identities are still tied in large part to our homes. Whether we are married or single, childless, career-oriented, or staying at home raising kids, there is still a part of our life's meaning that is tied to our homes. We, as women, still define ourselves in some way by the quality and quantity of work we do there.

By fully embracing Zen, the meaning of our life that is defined by our relationship to our homes ceases to be a burden. It becomes a joyous act that can shore us up when times are tough and reinforce all that is good about our lives in times of happiness and prosperity.

TRY THIS

Create a cleaning soundtrack for yourself. I loved the suggestion I got from a friend of listening to music while I was cleaning, so I tuned in to my favorite eighties station to give it a try. But just as I would be getting into the groove of a given task, a slow ballad would come on, or a song that reminded me of an ex-boyfriend, or a song that I found so annoying it would set my teeth on edge, and I'd have to stop what I was doing to change the tuner to another station, and the moment (and momentum) was gone. Instead, I burned a CD of peppy, fun, and upbeat songs that I can play at high decibels and dance around the house to as I clean. They improve my mood, they make me dance, and trick my mind into believing that I'm actually having fun. Download your favorite songs, design a fun label for them, and get busy. You might even have different soundtracks for different duties—for example, "Lauren's Laundry Folding Love Songs," or "Mopping with Madonna." Whatever makes you laugh! Laughter is the best medicine and it makes crummy jobs a lot more tolerable.

mantra for meditation on the use of rituals

May I learn to celebrate each and every moment and honor its importance.

haiku on rituals

celebrating life
its magic and mystery
moment by moment.

CONCLUSION

$\mathcal{I}$ set out on this path of Zen trying to learn an appreciation for the small things. I wanted to look at the past and I wanted to contemplate the future and figure out where I fit in the puzzle. I found lots of information and lots of answers. I am awed, in many ways, by the work of so many women, both the famous and the "ordinary," who have struggled to find meaning in their own lives and share it with the world. I feel a renewed sense of hope for my daughter and for other women who will face these challenges in the future. I also feel hope for my young son that perhaps he will marry and raise his children in a world that is more equitably balanced. I want him to be a full partner in the life of his family, and as we as a society are learning to be more respectful of our place on the planet, it can surely only follow that we will learn to respect each other more as well.

The thing I realized most of all during this process is that the answers do lie within me. I can no longer treat my life or my responsibilities as a joke—take my obligations lightly. I can overcome any challenge, be it biological, cultural, or psychological. I am making my own way in this world and it is up to me to make choices that will not stand in the way of progress but will foster growth and love and joy.

My life has been far more about the journey than the destination. I have always had goals and dreams, but I've never set myself a "be all, end all" point to achieve. I've just enjoyed accepting every challenge and seeing where things took me. As I mature, both chronologically and in my role as a wife and mother, I am beginning to lose some of that childlike immaturity and irresponsibility that has allowed me to let my environment be less than its best (to say the least). Examining Zen and trying to express its concepts on these pages has helped me to cement my divergent ideas about what it means to be a homemaker and the importance of keeping house. Whether or not my work is figured into the gross national product, I deserve to have a home that is peaceful and positive. My husband deserves it. My children deserve it.

For whatever reason, I have always had to take in a lot of information in order to make a decision. I can analyze the pros and cons of any situation for hours, days, and weeks at a time. I love to research and ponder. I love to ask the opinion of anyone willing to give it. I process all that "stuff" and then do exactly what *I* want to do! The reading, writing, and sharing of ideas that it has required to put this book together have inspired and energized me and convinced me to go forward—to do better, to be better, to continue working to overcome this challenge I have been fighting all my life. So many great women have gone before me. There is such a unique sisterhood of women out there right this very minute who understand exactly how I feel—both my joys and my frustrations, as well as yours. And there are lots of "little women" out there and women yet to be born who will continue to seek their place in this world. What it all boils down to for me is this: It's okay to seek and to strive. It's okay to feel alone every once in a while. It's okay to admit you are tired or bored. But it is an absolute necessity to eliminate things that are unnecessary and to find the essence of your life by surrounding yourself with people and things that are meaningful and to be excited about your life.

Poet T. S. Eliot wrote, "We shall not cease from exploration and the end of all our exploring will be to arrive where we started and know the place for the first time."

And so I find myself back at the beginning. Washing the dishes. I have been on an intellectual and emotional journey in creating this book. I have learned so much—about myself, about my friends and members of my family, about women who are complete strangers and yet have openly and honestly shared their feelings with me. I arrive back at this place with my eyes and my heart open. In many ways it is like knowing this place for the first time.

TRY THIS

Our exploration of Zen Housekeeping has been as much about changing our mindset as changing the way we do housework. The way we think about the work we do around our home is just as important as the work itself. Consider these words. Use them as a topic for meditation or as a cue for writing in your journal. Embrace them and integrate their meaning into your life each day: "Whatever is true, whatever is noble, whatever is right, whatever is pure, whatever is lovely, whatever is admirable—if anything is excellent or praiseworthy—think on these things."—Philippians 4:8

APPENDIX A.

RESOURCES

Gift From the Sea, by Anne Morrow Lindbergh—A memoir of self-discovery and an exploration of the ways in which a woman's life and relationships evolve over the course of her life.

Real Simple Magazine and *www.realsimple.com*—Fun, informative, and a treat for the eyes as well, with well-designed, colorful layouts. This Web site is filled with tips and suggestions from professionals as well as ordinary women.

The Undomestic Goddess, by Sophie Kinsella—This novel is a fun read for the domestically challenged. A high-powered professional finds herself unemployed and by accident takes on the job of live-in house-keeper to a wealthy family in the English countryside.

www.getgreenandclean.com—Web site for Shaklee products.

www.lighterfootstep.com—An entire Web site dedicated to a lifestyle based on sustainability. It offers a huge amount of information that makes the idea of transitioning to living green seem very possible.

www.lime.com—Healthy living with a twist.

www.momstown.com—This site was created by two moms, Mary Goulet and Heather Reider, who have been there, trying to face the personal challenges of being a mom and getting a life. They are also the authors of *The MomsTown Guide to Getting It All: A Life Makeover for Stay-at-Home Moms*, a fun book with great suggestions for reconnecting with the you that you were before you had children.

www.mops.org—A Web site for Mothers of Preschoolers.

www.mothersandmore.org—A Web site for "Sequencing" moms. One of the things I love about this organization is its efforts to turn moms into activists. There are a lot of us out here. If we would work together to lobby as a group instead of fighting "The Mommy Wars," we could potentially have a real impact on our society, the way businesses and government treat women and families, and more. Get involved.

www.organizedhome.com—A great resource for organizing every room in your house and every aspect of your life, with charts, worksheets, and more.

www.flylady.net—Great information, tips, etc., from a woman who has gone on her own journey of discovering how to clean house. Just one word of caution: The Fly Lady shares wonderful information and is very inspirational and motivational. However, if you sign up to receive her e-mail tips and reminders you will be bombarded with e-mail. It may be extremely beneficial to you to have constant reminders, but you will receive literally hundreds of e-mails in a very short period of time.

www.theknot.com—This site is intended for newlyweds but is rich in resources for all of us on making and keeping a house and building strong relationships.

www.thezensite.com—Extremely informative about many aspects of Zen with links to absolutely everything related to Zen.

www.treehugger.com—Wanna get green? Start here. Tons of ways you can contribute to a happier, healthier planet

Opportunity for Existential Extra Credit on the Path to Enlightenment

I admit it. I was the dork who always loved school and took every opportunity to get extra credit. And in my opinion, there should be opportunities for extra credit along the path to Enlightenment. If such an opportunity exists, it would have to be in tackling the really tough jobs like these.

Cleaning and Organizing the Garage

Many of us have so much stuff in our garage that we can no longer even utilize it for its intended purpose—to park our cars! The garage was designed to protect cars from the elements, keep them safe, and serve as a conduit between the outside world and the inside of our homes. Instead, it has become a dumping ground for lawn and sports equipment, extra furniture we don't want to keep but for some reason can't seem to part with, bags that never made it to Goodwill, extra air filters . . . anything and everything that we need on a fairly regular basis but just don't know what to do with!

How do we tackle the disorder and return our garages to their intended purpose?

- Your first step is either to dispose of or find a better, safer place for chemicals, gasoline, paint—items that could be toxic or create safety hazards.

- Next, ruthlessly get rid of items that you will never use again. Get the bags of clothes and books as well as the extra furniture you are never going to use to Goodwill. In many communities, charitable organizations will come and pick up donated items from you, eliminating yet one more excuse for why you can't get the stuff out of the garage.

- Check that any tools that are stored in the garage have all their parts and are actually still functional. If not, either get them to a repair shop or get rid of them. Many organizations will also accept donations of broken appliances, provide someone in need with the job of repairing them, and then resell them. Look in your phone book for contact information on organizations with these types of programs.

- Invest in some high-quality, durable hooks that were designed to hold heavy items and place them at intervals down one wall of the garage. These can be used to hang up rakes, shovels, and other gardening tools. Lawn chairs can be kept out of the way.

- High-grade hooks hung from the ceiling can serve as places to hang bicycles to keep them out of the way. There are also harnesses designed specifically for this purpose that can be installed directly onto the wall.
- Next, purchase a shelving unit or two for storage of all other items. It is a good idea to anchor these units to the wall so that they do not fall over or get pulled over. You should also place the heaviest items on bottom shelves and place the lighter items toward the top so that shelves do not become top-heavy.
- Store all sports equipment together in a large plastic bin.

Following these steps will ensure that your garage provides easy access to necessary tools and equipment and that your automobiles can return to their rightful homes.

CLEANING AND ORGANIZING THE ATTIC

Attics are treasure-troves of stuff that we want to keep out of sight, and therefore it stays out of mind. Often you forget what you've even put up there. You just keep pushing more and more cardboard boxes into the space until you couldn't find anything even if you wanted to. Remember the Zen concept of *miegakure*? The concept that just because something isn't visible doesn't mean it's not there? This concept is directly applicable to the attic. We don't see the things that are hidden away up there, but we know that they are there. The presence of junk even if it is hidden can interfere with the flow of chi and impair the good karma that we have worked so hard to achieve in cleaning our home. Don't let the attic stand between you and enlightenment!

Step-by-step attic attack plan:

- First, get everything out of the attic.
- Go through each box with the decluttering tips you've already learned in mind and throw away everything that is not absolutely necessary.
- Replace cardboard boxes with large, clear plastic containers.
- Create a theme for each container or place like items with like items. The hodgepodge of stuff that we usually store in the boxes we place in the attic makes accessing something that we need quickly and easily a virtual impossibility.
- Label each container. You can make each description as long or as short as you like as long as you understand what you've written. Remember you are trying to transform your attic from land of the lost to a valuable storage location.
- With your attic empty, take a look around and see what space you do have there.
- Create zones in the space. For example, in the back right-hand corner you will store all holiday decorations. The back left-hand corner will be the location for sporting equipment.
- The more infrequent the use, the further to the back a container can reside.

- Return your organized and well-identified containers to their zone in the attic space.
- Turn off the light, close the door, and pat yourself on the back for a really difficult job well done.

CLEANING AND ORGANIZING THE BASEMENT

Depending on what part of the country you live in, your basement may serve a variety of purposes. We live in the part of the country known as tornado alley, so our basement is actually called a storm cellar where we are supposed to retreat in the event that a twister comes sweeping down the plain. In the northeast, basements serve as the nerve center of many homes. The basement is where the heating and cooling units are located and often the washer and dryer as well. It is often a popular home remodeling upgrade to enclose and "finish" the basement, making it an extra bedroom, playroom, or office. In some parts of the country basements are not even considered necessary or are impossible to create due to the geographical makeup of the land and are not included in homes. And due to the high cost of creating them, many homebuilders no longer include basements in home design. But if you do have a basement, there are some ideas you ought to keep in mind as you go about getting and keeping it organized.

- Due to its location below ground level, basements can flood. Even in the driest of climates a freak heavy rainstorm could potentially be devastating.

- Do not store chemicals of any kind in your basement.
- Keep a heavy-duty flashlight at the top of the basement stairs in the event of a power outage.
- Clear clutter from the areas around any appliances housed in your basement. You do not want to create a fire hazard and you want to be able to get to them when they need maintenance or repairs.
- If you use your basement for storage, utilize the same types of bins we used for the attic and store them in a similar fashion—like items together, clearly labeled, in specific zones.
- Make sure there is plenty of shelving and storage, and utilize it.

You have now tackled the three toughest jobs your home has to offer. Maintain the organization of these spaces and they will be tremendous assets to you. You are also well on your way to nirvana!

APPENDIX C.

HOUSEKEEPING TRIVIA

Government studies report that the average person living in the United States spends $75 annually on 20,805 sheets of toilet paper. The average person uses 57 sheets of toilet paper per day. Who knew? I never thought to count!

Ancient Egyptians were the first people to bathe, cleaning their skin with oils, around 1500 B.C.

Due to the abundance of natural hot springs as well as cultural and religious rituals, the Japanese have held bathing in high regard throughout their history.

Egyptians were also the first folks to use bleach and around 3000 B.C. were known to produce beautiful white linen from brown fabric. Maybe this is why Egyptian cotton sheets are still so highly valued.

Bon Ami was the first powdered cleanser, introduced to homemakers in 1886. Sand, chalk, quartz, pumice, and petrified wood were the first ingredients added to give the cleanser its abrasive quality.

Over 4,000 years ago, Minoan royalty used a flushing toilet. What the heck took us so long to incorporate that invention?

SOS Pads were invented by the wife of a door-to-door pots and pans salesman. What does SOS stand for? Save Our Saucepans!

The vacuum cleaner is only 100 years old, invented when janitor James Murray Spangler attached a motor to a soap box, used a pillow case as a dust trap, and stapled the contraption to a broom handle. Now that's using your resources. They could make a vacuum cleaner to use on *Survivor* with some coconuts and bamboo!

The first garbage disposal was invented in 1927 by John Hammes. After perfecting his product, he started a company called InSinkErator. If you take a look, I bet your kitchen disposal is still made by InSinkErator. Mine is!

Over 500 patents for apple/potato peelers were issued during the 1800s.

Saran Wrap, or actually the substance that it is made from, was discovered by accident in 1933 by a worker at Dow Chemicals named Ralph Wiley. The substance was found to be darn near indestructible and was initially used as a coating on seagoing airplanes during World War II to protect them from the corrosive properties of the salt water. Saran Wrap as we know it first became available for use in the home in 1953.

APPENDIX D.

QUICK REFERENCE FOR
ZEN TERMS AND CONCEPTS

Dukkha—the human condition known as suffering.

Eightfold Path—Guidelines for living that will help to ease suffering.
These guidelines are the substance of the fourth noble truth of Zen.
They include:

Right understanding

Right thought

Right speech

Right action

Right livelihood

Right effort

Right mindfulness

Right concentration

Feng shui—literally translated as "wind and water," feng shui is the Chinese study of the placement and arrangement of objects in order to maximize the flow of chi through a given space.

Five Hindrances—psychological factors that stand between you and enlightenment, including:

Desire

Anger

Sloth

Worry

Doubt

Four Noble Truths—These were the revelations that Buddha experienced that led him to enlightenment.

Haiku—A form of Japanese poetry that adheres to a three-line format with the first line containing five syllables, the second line containing seven syllables, and the third line returning to five syllables. The focus of a haiku is to capture a specific moment free of restriction.

Kanso—Simplicity.

Karma—The universal law of cause and effect. What people do, for better or for worse, will revisit them, whether in this life or in another incarnation.

Kinhin—Walking meditation.

Mantra—A sound, word, or phrase uttered repeatedly to serve as a point of focus during meditation.

Meditation—A state of relaxed awareness, the practice of which can lead one to revelations of universal truths.

Miegakure—Defined as the avoidance of full expression, the concept of miegakure expresses that although something may not be entirely visible, it doesn't detract from the importance of the whole.

Origami—Art of paper folding.

Seven Factors of Enlightenment—Enlightenment-related states or ideals that can be topics for meditation and right living. The seven factors of enlightenment are:

Investigation

Tranquility

Mindfulness

Concentration

Energy

Equanimity

Rapture

Shizen—Naturalness.

Shosin—Beginner's mind.

Zazen—Seated meditation.

Zendo—A Zen meditation hall.

HOUSEKEEPING JOURNAL